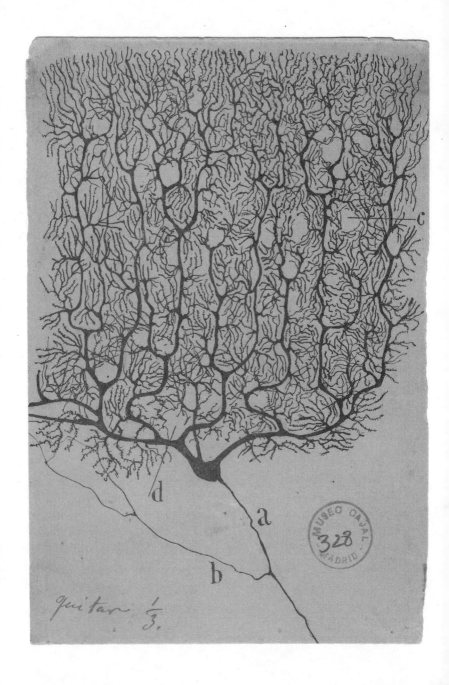

c

d

a

b

guitar ⅓.

ALL THE FIERCE TETHERS

ESSAYS

LIA PURPURA

SARABANDE BOOKS
Louisville, KY

Library of Congress Cataloging-in-Publication Data
Names: Purpura, Lia – author.
Title: All the fierce tethers : essays / by Lia Purpura.
Description: First edition. | Louisville, KY : Sarabande Books, 2018.
Identifiers: LCCN 2018007725 (print) | LCCN 2018011823 (e-book)
ISBN 9781946448316 (e-book) | ISBN 9781946448309 (pbk. : alk. paper)
Classification: LCC PS3566.U67 (ebook)
LCC PS3566.U67 A6 2018 (print) | DDC 814/.54—DC23
LC record available at https://lccn.loc.gov/2018007725

Cover image: *Purkinje Cell of the human cerebellum. Golgi method. a, axón; b,
recurrent colateral; c and d, spaces in the dendritic arborization for stellate cells.*
Original drawing by Santiago Ramón y Cajal,
black Chinese ink on paper, c. 1899. Courtesy of the Cajal Institute–
Spanish National Research Council (CSIC), Madrid, Spain. © CSIC.

Cover and interior design by Alban Fischer.
Manufactured in Canada.
This book is printed on acid-free paper.
Sarabande Books is a nonprofit literary organization.

This project is supported in part by the National Endowment for
the Arts. The Kentucky Arts Council, the state arts agency, supports
Sarabande Books with state tax dollars and federal funding from the
National Endowment for the Arts.

TO MY MOTHER AND FATHER

CONTENTS

ALL THE FIERCE TETHERS

SCREAM (OR NEVER MINDING)

There are things I'm supposed to never mind. "Never mind" means *silent* and *agreed upon* and that I must want, more than anything, to get through the day and so should assent to go along. Glance. Turn the page. Turn away from a scream, and the place from which a scream would rise, if cultivated by attention paid.

Subjects one might avoid: ruined land, ruined animals. Because the issues of the day can begin to feel old, and people get tired of feeling bad.

When I was a child I was not daunted. I let myself get completely exhausted.

Never minding makes it possible to do things like eat what you want, and talk about simple, daily things.

A scream is not speech.

Edvard Munch's *The Scream* was recently sold for nearly 120 million dollars. He called it "a cry from the heart," and wrote about it to a friend, "I was being stretched to the limit—nature was screaming in my blood—I was at breaking point . . ." But as a gesture performed over and over, on coffee mugs, tote bags, key chains, and cards, it's much reduced, quieted so as to be understood. Seeing *The Scream* again and again, we agree not to.

Instead, we refer to.

Consider all we throw away. The tin my mints came in could do so much work. Could be put to good use and serve again, holding buttons, coins, pills. Then fewer tins would have to be made. Imagine (though there's no need to, this is all real) how many things are made to be thrown away. You can't care about them. Their brevity isn't meaningful, like, say, a dart with a poisoned tip, a spear, an arrowhead—objects whose single use sustains.

Yes, I understand making tins is a job. A way of making a living. That people have jobs making trash for a living.

That subs, heroes, or grinders, whatever they're called, are sold by the inch. That drinks are called "bottomless." That for a set price you can eat all night, stack BBQ ribs ten inches high if you balance just right, heading back to your seat.

What a deal that is.

If more is the measure, if the point is *a lot*—best not to fuss over the origins of stuff. And, too, if origins are questionable, you'd want the distance between farm and table to be as vast as possible. Vast is stable. Ribs are tasty. I mean a *factory* farm. A Concentrated Animal Feeding Operation. A CAFO. An acronym is a form of speed, a way to fly past the origin of an idea. Kellogg's Concentrate was my favorite cereal as a kid. I liked it, too, for its double meaning—a dense substance/a command to think hard. Here, though, "Concentrated" means: twenty hogs in a space the size of your bedroom; ten chickens in a two-foot-square pen—that's an area the size of this page for each chicken. Under such conditions, animals are driven mad.

I probably don't have to be so direct here.

I'm sure you've heard a lot about this.

Once, a bandwagon was used for exactly that purpose: to carry musicians in a procession. To "jump on" one now means *to join a successful enterprise*. So many forms of success depend on never minding, on taking the steps two at a time, up to the wagon, and climbing on for the ride. Or think of riding a tide: a force absorbs you, purpose transports, and a shared mind washes over.

At the edges, though—near jetties and inlets, in dips and depressions—little tide pools settle and still, and that's where the interesting stuff collects. You have to get down on your knees to see all the briny, colloidal, fast-swimming creatures that, at a distance, look only like murk.

I want to think about #419.

What might seem like veering around here, isn't. I'm trying to lay in how many times a day, and in how many ways, a person—I— might turn away.

Or else, what—stay and scream?

Solastalgia is a very good word, made by combining the Latin *solacium* (comfort) and the Greek root *algia* (pain). Philosopher Glenn Albrecht created it to define "the pain experienced when the place one loves and where one resides is under assault." I'm working on a word for *the loss of fellow feeling for a creature and the strange emptiness such a loss leaves in its place*. *Zoosympenia* might do. *Zoo* (animal) + *sym* (feeling) + *penia* (loss). But first, before words, a feeling must root. For me, it was winter, late afternoon, when eye level with the stove—a beautiful old Chambers—I'd set things in motion. The oven door had a hooked lever which, fixed between two orange dials, made it into the face of an owl. It was possible to come around the corner unseen, inch up to the bird, flip its beak, hear it talk, touch its ever-open eyes. Say "hi" in passing, or play in its gaze. Nearby was a horse in the linoleum. A horse's *head* to be more precise, a little disconcerting, but like a ragged cloud shape in the sky, more a suggestion than a truncated thing. The horse had its own scent when I laid my head next to it. We talked in the mornings. It was always ready. I also had a collection of bees, paper ones my mother cut from tuna cans, and distributed on alternate weeks to me and my sister. We'd toss them in air and watch them sift down on the flowers we were.

When I was four, the world was ending. I couldn't be certain. I just suspected. It was 1968 and the war was on. I had a dog, a monkey, a fox. I did not think of them as toys. If the world was a storm, I was an ark.

I'll get to work on another word, too—something for *the loss of relationship to singular objects due to an overabundance of them.*

How about: *Aesthesioplegia. Aesthesio* (sensation) + *plegia* (paralysis).

To understand an object's habits, its tricks, you have to live with it daily. A milk bottle (the one I grew up with had a high, cinched waist and a full-skirted body) might let you take an illegal swig, but only if you used both hands. You might blue the last inch of milk by holding it up to the morning sun and tipping it almost horizontal.

Endless abundance clobbers the chance for relationships. So for example, if asked *Would you like to help stop wrecking the earth?* you'd say, of course, *Yes.* If asked, then, to drink only from water fountains and never again buy a bottle of water . . . well, it's hard to imagine giving up convenience—though what you'd get, in return, is the chance to learn the quirks of your local fountains: the cold ones with high arcs, the calmer but warmer, dribbly ones. You might choose to walk further for the beautiful, pebbly fountain, or make do with closer, slightly tin-flavored water. Or you might carry your own collapsible cup (I had one as a Girl Scout), which when folded would be exactly the size of a tin of mints.

#419 is a cow; that's a tag in its ear. There's a #308 right behind it, a #376, and a #454 all jammed in the frame of the photo. This must be a mixed lot. If I stand back just a little or, rather, hold the newspaper out at arm's length and unfocus a bit, the numbers fade and the cows are wearing bell-shaped earrings. If I shut my eyes, and shut many more things—doors in the brain—if I conjure up Heidi and green fields and milk pails, I can hear the little cowbells tinkling. And see the concrete outside my door roll up like a rug, cartoon-style, revealing the sleeping pasture below. Which reconstitutes in sun and springs with fat flowers back to life. And feeds all the cows on endless, rollicking, cartoon greens.

A *Starry Night* mug. A Caillebotte trivet. *Mona Lisa* fridge magnets. Cézanne wrapping paper.

419 is bending to eat. Not grass but corn. I guess I should say *eating what she's made to eat* which likely includes swine manure, poultry feathers, cement dust, and plastic for roughage. All cheaper and more efficient than grass, easily supplied in confined spaces—though contributing, as you might imagine, to conditions that justify prophylactic antibiotics. But let me just do a description here. Establish a scene. 419 is bending to eat. Her tags are clearly visible, as is the patch of white between her eyes, which are good at seeing blue-purples and yellow-greens and not so adept at the red-brown-pink spectrum. And there, in relief, against the white chest of 308—the fringe of 419's black eyelashes. Like a girl's. Like my son's in sleep.

Once you really see a thing (even briefly, and slight as a lash) it's hard to unsee.

This summer I saw two sandpipers dig for crabs at the edge of the shore with long, pointed beaks. When the waves rolled out, one dug, picked, and ate very quickly. The other plucked its catch and ran straight to a dry spot higher up and took its time pecking every bit of meat. One found more crabs, but ate each only partly. The other stuck with a single crab and mined it completely. One was not more adept, or the other wiser—just that, there, undeniably, was the inclination each had. It was impossible to miss: each preferred its own method, each had an idea, a disposition. A sensibility. An imagination.

Endless *Starry Night*s wreck time. *Great Wave*s get drained, and *Sunflowers* dimmed by repetition. What Munch once made of a sensation at dusk (his friends having left him after a walk, his brief pause on the path and growing despair) is no longer a space where you and the painter might linger together. Now it's a trinket. A T-shirt. A necklace. A thing you stop seeing that stands in for. It's a joke. A tactic. A way to connect at the office, in meetings (which make everyone want to scream). A while back, inflatable *Scream* dolls were all the rage—there on your desk, or life-sized, a bald, angsty friend who'd commiserate, lift a beer with you at the end of the day. Imagine him on the label of a microbrew—the colors amped, the border crisp. A beer called Scream. Scream lager. Scream ale.

I'd like to think the painting's new owner wanted back to a

time before the image refracted, to park a chair near the original sky, the fat blue scream pressing in like a wave, the bridge's red rail like an iron poker, the gash of sky marbled and fleshy, and to be, as everything was—clouds, air, nerves, smudgy suggestion of boats—overcome. I'm hoping he wanted to clear some space, amid colors eddying fast and draining, so a scream might speak, singularly, to him.

To own a thing in a more perfect way, go into training. Adopt the gestures of a beloved friend you rarely see, the way she holds a thought in her hands and twists it into place in air. Study how her fingers flare when describing something unjust, or a point beyond which she won't be pushed, so you, too, can shape ideas in air and better span the distance between you.

Or, paring a spot of mold from cheese, take up a worn, well-sharpened knife, and cutting slowly toward your body, let the blade come to rest against the flesh of your thumb—and in this, the old-fashioned way, freehand, with no cutting board— spend a few moments with your grandmother again.

Some forms of ownership don't require the purchase of anything.

I'm meant to forget that certain very basic gestures—fingers on toggles—are a satisfaction, and to never mind their passing. Am I alone in wanting to turn and adjust faucet handles? Repair fixtures with a wrench and a smear of putty? Yank those old restroom towels-on-rollers to produce a clean spot? Now you need only wave your wet hands at a sensor or move around until lasers kick in. Or often, don't. And then there you are, swaying dumbly alone in your stall—a scene very different than, say, a man dancing naked, as William Carlos Williams wrote,

> grotesquely
> before my mirror
> waving my shirt round my head
> and singing softly to myself:
> "I am lonely, lonely"

—a loneliness so vital it's worth celebrating, so human and achy it calls forth the drive to make something of it.

Or how about this: You've got a drill with a bad battery, a nickel-cadmium, heavy-metal thing you want to recycle. Opening the drill takes a good ten minutes with tiny screwdrivers. The drill itself is just fine, the gears enmeshed and sharp, the motor precise in its cylindrical compactness and nestled within its casing, all the parts able to perform. But the battery pack costs way more than the drill, is specialized and hard to find, or doesn't even exist without the drill, so you throw the whole thing away.

A thing designed with a subsystem that quits, with no way of keeping the still-working parts. An object lost to itself at the outset. No sense of a tool becoming, through long use, a hand's extension, no hint of its shape responding to a body—of such a fit being intimate.

I'm not supposed to be upset by any of this.

Childhood's a long training in never minding all you're los-
ing, everything that's falling, crashing, being taken. In the dia-
monded, rhinestoned late 1970s most things were too bright,
or tight, or Lucite—and I wasn't learning. I turned away from
(and here's a good, bygone word) the *boughten*, and instead
toward—mostly a dream of wildness, Long Island's marshes
filled in and blacktopped for parking lots, malls, and Levittowns.
I spent much time prospecting for bits. One summer I rose at
dawn and gathered dandelions from all the front yards, washed
and sugared them, added yeast, water, lemon—and then, for
the next few weeks, set to racking off my dandelion wine. (I was
reading Bradbury's story at the time.) I wore flannel shirts and
overalls, work boots and braids. In love with my bike and my
dog, I read outdoor survival guides and looked for occasions to
use the word "pemmican." I wrote out the steps for tanning hides
(the native way, with animal brains, or ash, or acorns), heard
"mall" as the tool—not as a baubly, overlit place. What others
called "wild" in me I knew to be a fending off. A countering. A
minding greatly.

In the Outdoors section of the *Rapid City Journal*, I recently read
about a couple "Bonded by Their Adventures." Their twenty
safaris. Their thirty-year marriage. A few of their tales were
gathered therein (in the scary dark of a rainforest when etc. etc.
which ended in "the pure joy of being together outdoors")—but

it was the photo that held me. On the very bright walls, head after head (after head after head)—at least fifty mounts in the living room alone. And how strange the couple looked, alive, among them.

I remember the busts of Beethoven and Mozart (and Haydn and Liszt and Chopin) in my elementary school's music room. I couldn't make any sense of them: a pianist with no arms, a joyless composer who wrote "Ode to Joy." Their limbless bodies in marbly coldness. Stunted and chopped. I knew a head with a bit of neck was meant to be never minded. Another version of how-things-are-done. The men, canonical. The sculptures, memorial. I *understood*.

Still, it was hard to see anything but severedness.

You should know that the place in *The Scream* where the figure stands is an actual road in Oslo overlooking the bay where screams from the slaughterhouse and asylum converged. Munch's sister was locked in there, while he was free to walk with friends and think and listen and create.

He wrote:

I went along the road with two friends—
The sun set
Suddenly the sky became blood—and I felt the breath of sadness
A tearing pain beneath my heart
I stopped—leaned against the fence—deathly tired
Clouds over the fjord of blood dripped, reeking blood

My friends went on but I just stood trembling with an open wound in my breast ~~trembling with anxiety~~ I heard a huge extraordinary scream pass through nature.

You might try it—anyone might: at the end of a day finding yourself abruptly alone, and since certain sounds cannot be unheard, certain images cannot be unseen, in that moment, when a bay might tilt, or a sky drain and pin its red light hard to your chest, you might press your hands to your ears, and, at that spot where the world leaks in, wherever it happens—diner, store, street—there, in the moment a scream originates, try to make something of that.

ON PHOTOGRAPHING CHILDREN IN TREES

The pros are out with their props and equipment—wipes for the sap and the acorn stains, noisemaking toys and funny balloons, so eyes up and look here!—that it might seem the kids aren't arranged, the trees not decorative, and a girl is called out of real reverie, a tree-climbing haze, to be photographed for a holiday card then released. As if the light around the trees were not amped by big reflective screens, and the trees not mind posing as Nature, garland, or frame. Such is the dream of pastoral time, free and unmanaged here in the park, preserved by a child in the fat crown of an oak, still green, no gold roughing in, no falling yet, it isn't fall yet, just very high summer suspended.

It looks like that tree might be *her* tree—where she goes to hear herself speak, tree demanding no words, but tender in the space between nose and bark (scent of pond water, cinnamon, musk)—where ants on their village roads haul their bundles in strict, ordered lines. From where I'm standing, I can see her trying—how to admit those whose voices and bodies disrupt the clear ant-thoughts that touch her deep in and call her to breathe a warm safety-cloud over their fear.

The trees of my childhood? Both yard-bound and wild,

holding their street corners, shadows, birdsong. A mimosa, whose pinfeather blossoms grew into explosions that held on for weeks, then unpinked and puddled up brown in the driveway—and the double-take, heart-slash when just recently I heard it called a *trash tree*, as strange and world-tilting as learning someone you loved and thought funny, irreverent, so fully alive (as maybe you'd be if lucky, when grown) was *a drunk* at all those parties. And still you keep on with your love's bright refusals. The crab apple: my father cut a branch after it split in a storm and made my mother a cane from it, bowed in the center like a leg with rickets, but she loved it and refused the upright steel one. The fishing tree—what my son called the dogwood where he and my father played their games, and which for me early on could be petted, called to, and fed. And central in my grandmother's patch of backyard, the white birch, its cool skin so pink and damp when I laid my hand on it, whose job it was to shade the devotionals, her tomatoes and roses, prize-winning if she'd been after prizes, lavished with care, tended in the small space available here in the new world. I was no immigrant, but the birch and I spoke like a couple who, from different countries, used a third language between them.

It has always been so on holiday cards: backlit child on a swing at sunset; or at the shore, poking a starfish with a shy finger, or handed a flower to sniff for innocence—or as it is today, just across from the park, a sister and brother in matching white shirts, posed on a bench on a rolling green lawn with arms cued around each others' shoulders, meaning love (more a respite from fighting if you'd seen them before they got yelled at). Four times a year, on the white-shirted kids' lawn, up go the yellow warning flags, with person and dog figures X'd out and a date written in when it'll be safe again to play, the poison absorbed and the excess washed off into the bay. Before the family moved in last year, ivy tangled up the stone walls and darkened the mossy root folds of old maples. At the edge of their property was a tremendous magnolia, an extravagance I'd cross three neighborhoods to see. It was crawl-space private underneath and smelled of iron-mud-worms. Its blooms were made of milk and blood, fire and cream. After a few weeks, they tore out every-thing green, cut down the magnolia, and rolled lengths of sod over the graded yard and around the stump like a bunched, bulky scarf. The cut tree sent out buds, then shoots, came partly back as a magnolia bush, and maybe would've been more, but a stump grinder finished it off.

All this for a lawn where no kids play but get propped and cajoled, instructed in poise, which means to please, to be pleas-ing—which is someone else's need, not yours, and you'll have to fight that too, dear girl in a tree refusing to look at the camera and smile, you who'd rather go dark, hands cupped like horse blinders, face in the bark so one single ray at a time is admitted and shines on the sap where a stuck ant part meets you deep in, where something's now blowing across the lake of my chest, loosening my ribs, all my parts slipping and I'm no more-than, just bigger-than ant, very softened beneath my skin, light sharp on that bit of ant body (and I'm sorry, always—why sorry? For seeing?), while the whole and intact ants file over the rough bark, so when I look up inside my head where the colors come and snap and burst, the parts that are broken ride themselves back into the black night's full body.

ENTRY COVE

I say *entry cove* in ignorance, to name the world as I can, make-shift, by a phrase that lights on the skin—*entry cove*, a space made in tall grass and darted through, sound enough to constitute a hideaway in a meadow. A cove is generous in definition: a sheltering bay, a cave, gap, or hollow. As I near, an animal slower and heavier than a cat slips in. *Cove*, because I want to follow, everything outside too loud and wrong.

Here at the edge of this meadow, late summer, the goldenrod high, the sun warm and air soft, there's a motor, compressor, something violently chewing the quiet, shredding the peace. Hard to locate its origin. Overhead, a plane tears a path into blue sky. Then comes a far train whistle I make romantic to alter the imposition—until it turns back to the truck horn it is and I'm recomposed, on the outskirts again, making do.

You asked for my impression, you who once lived in this ruined town for years. After just a few days, I'm so hungry I'll take anything green. I sift for green moments, accept reduced portions, this circumscribed loop. Some stretches are fine: rows of stables repurposed as offices, all the worn, silvery boards intact. Near a once-barn, there's a real footbridge arcing over a trickle of creek. And this meadow-reprieve, preserve, conscious allotment of wild—it helps.

It was a woodchuck, I can see now. She's out and settled on the shorn path, fully adapted to the machinery noise, no wincing or twitching, just nibbling grass. As I move closer, she slips back into the green tangle. Then we do it again: I circle the meadow, and coming around, she's out on the path. I close in, she retreats—only partly though, now that she knows it's me. And just as she's wagered, I do move along. There's a name for me and the distance I keep. That I can't know it doesn't mean that I'm not, at this moment, being addressed.

Though I grew up across the street from a parking lot, it did at least lead to a small county park and a lake—my fancy, my scrap, really, only a pond. Half the pond was belted by a paved path and half was left wooded. Whole stretches had their microclimates, each distinct and brief as a shiver, or a stripe of afternoon sun in the eyes. At the path's beginning was a rocky area where fat white Long Island ducks gathered for handouts. Then a sadder stretch, treeless and too-bright, with splintery pilings where old men sat and fished in the murk. Then a relief-stretch where the pilings stopped and scrubby grass ran down to the water, willows shaded the banks, and the year-round geese slept. On the far side of the pond before the woods started was a rise, an open, mowed area I tried to believe in for years, thought could be used, it should have been used, made productive, *trod*, *tilled*, or *encamped*—but such language wasn't available to me, *plots* went undrawn, we weren't a *village*, there wasn't a *harvest*, we had dirt and not *soil*, and no one had *earth*. The space felt shunned—not left-to-reverence, not sacred-kept—and I couldn't get it to breathe or work or activate. Heading up there was an obligation, an attempt to restore I couldn't say what. Most days I'd focus past it, move quickly and try not to feel its need. The path ended in a turnaround, and beyond that loop, with its garbage cans, snarls of fishing line, rusty hooks, was the fence to the woods, called "the Pit" by the neighborhood kids. But it wasn't a pit. It was never a quarry. It had no maw. There was no town legend telling its origin. By *pit* they meant only the interval—filler, like TV snow at the end of the dial—before entertainment resolved again.

If I felt like testing my footing, I'd climb out and swing around the fence, which leaned far into the water; usually, I'd just go over, get in fast and head to the steep, embrambled part, vast-feeling and furthest from home. So few were the raw places I could get to, spots no words touched, where language unhinged. And here, though the land had no name or story, I could read in the rock-cluster broods how light grew long and patted them, or touched the tallest tree-crowns so briefly. Ground gave. Wind found the undersides of leaves. Each spot was full of explanations—not answers exactly, I came with no questions—but still, ferns sprung into feather, the spines of fish and big-eyed skulls of birds bent me to them. The midway-through part was bright and exposed, so I moved fast there, past the rusty No Trespassing signs, eye tuned for turtles and snakes—the neat holes of almost-never-seen snakes—so I could confirm my own ways of hiding.

Then, coming fully around, there was the neighborhood side again, marked by another fence where I sat and waited for fish to surface, or a turtle to clarify on a log. Usually, after a rest, I turned and went back in for another dose. Though I knew nothing but the most basic tree names and a couple of grasses, that soft greens went by *moss* and floating greens *algae*, I applied these to the damage "the Pit" had done. I went alone. I didn't want to play at hiding or being chased, or pass through quickly en route to some other activity. I wanted no chat to scuff the sounds of other lives. It wasn't a forest, it wasn't a marsh. I didn't measure or think in acres. It was the one place I had where land went rightful. Where I could finally stop converting.

With certain habits of mind engaged, ruin can be altered or even dissembled. Say I lived in upstate New York, say—Niagara. The chronic, anxious hum of traffic might be recast: *That's just the Falls*. Industrial grinding: *Just the Falls*. Flightpath: *Falls*. Off-loading: *Falls*. I've long been in the business of converting, though not all cases are difficult ones. Some are sidelong or slant; sometimes the shift is agile-feeling, and not employed to salve or deflect. So a dark bank of late afternoon clouds might become mountains-at-sunset, plunging us into valley life: Baltimore at the foot of a range, the Cascades (in my car driving west into the city, I speak it, *Cascades*, that open, then tumbling, icy *a*, delicious double-click *c* outcropping), and the air goes hazy with snow-mist, the word *foothills* makes all worn things feel glacier-rubbed. How good to be, at the end of the day, overseen by something majestic. Or, in a childhood act of conversion, I could turn dim-winter-solitude to street-gaslit-by-Leerie, Leerie in his big brown coat who worked his patch of London at dusk with ladder and torch and waved to children having their tea, for whom I waited page after page, my own torch lighting my book in bed.

For a long while I called the churn of waves back home *old lace* and the rich biotic foam *bright spun* along the Long Island shore, until that wouldn't work anymore, and leaks or spills, which sound benign, household even, meant it was time to recast the froth—make it no longer of light and air, and not dissolvable, but dire. In this way a childhood ends—that is, some tactics no longer work.

Some things are impossible to convert: What are trees with all their limbs cut? Mute stubs or thumbs. A field of pins. A hill of blunts. A very complete desolation. No right mind would draw a forest where a bird couldn't land, make the space leafless so the wind couldn't speak. *After a fire* is the best I can do—but a good burn doesn't work that way, and I can't slide a clearcut along the converter, ruin carried along the moving belt of my hope. My urban versions are just as helpless: heaps of clothing, lamps, mattresses, TVs at the curb? Not the chaos of moving, but *eviction*. And bright spots in alleys? Not sun hitting puddles, but needles among the broken glass.

Real change, not conversion, abounds. It does. Here's a branchful of yellow on a still-green oak in the meadow, late summer, an actual herald, a season called in, not something to be reconfigured, in need of being eased or staunched. And the luminous parchment shells of cicadas, husks of sycamore, and black locust pods I step on for the crunch—all forms en route to their proper end. No need to see with a strategy, with habits employed to keep back the grief which, anyway, overruns the banks I make.

You told me it would be desolate here; I suspect it's gotten worse since you left—the downtown's nearly abandoned now, its main street stretched wide by emptiness, no one out for a little air, no one meeting up for lunch. The tattoo parlors, cheap bars, and salons are brief stops along the interstate. Such loss makes any-one just-passing-through move along faster. Dusk here might be convertible if—no, let me stop. Dusk might be unto itself, if the light's allowed to catch a breath, its roughness held against the body of a warehouse, loading dock, trailer, if the scene it colors has no name but I let the light work and the scene stays uncaptioned, purples and softens, iron peels like bark, like skin, every underside reddens and the oily puddles iridesce and I'm in, nowhere else, and it's awful, it isn't, and I don't want to stay, and I stay with it.

MY EAGLES

My first eagle: South Dakota, Highway 385 out of Deadwood, late morning, November. I was hoping for it, since I'd never seen one before. My friend slowed the car and pointed up and said, "There's your eagle." At first, I heard "seagull" (I grew up on Long Island and gulls are all over) but the shape wouldn't clarify—too much hook, too much curve—and I fast reheard "eagle." In my pocket was a quarter, which later that day I'd resee as an amulet, a way to keep belief near: *E pluribus unum*, "Out of many, one" (the words sit like a hat on our eagle's head), likely a variation on a fragment by Heraclitus: "Out of all things, one, and one out of all things." As a slogan it predates "The melting pot," which in my child's eye I saw as an actual kettle suffering a too-high heat, collapsing, forming a molten puddle—impossible to unimagine now, and which somehow meant *my country*.

Flying low over the highway, the bird was so close it had actual feathers (not embossed, not etched) and a neck it turned to better see us. Or not us, but whatever it might clean up, pick at, side of the highway, freshly killed. Either way, as it angled its head, feathers parted and there was a gap, a tender dark spot where a little chill must have hit, as it does for me when I turn a corner and the wind lifts my hair, finds my neck, and slips in.

*

Ben Franklin didn't think much of the eagle. (*Bald*, by the way, is from *piebald*—two-colored, the white head and tail against the dark body.) He wrote, in a well-known letter to his daughter:

> For my own part, I wish the Bald Eagle had not been chosen as the Representative of our Country. He is a Bird of bad moral Character. He does not get his Living honestly. You may have seen him perched on some dead Tree near the River, where, too lazy to fish for himself, he watches the Labour of the Fishing Hawk; and when that diligent Bird has at length taken a Fish, and is bearing it to his Nest for the Support of his Mate and young Ones, the Bald Eagle pursues him and takes it from him.
>
> With all this injustice he is never in good case, but like those among men who live by sharping & robbing, he is generally poor and often very lousy. Besides, he is a rank coward: The little King Bird not bigger than a Sparrow attacks him boldly and drives him out of the district.

*

My second eagle came forth as a feather. A friend showed it to me, lifting the lid of the cedar box where she kept it, where I wasn't sure it wanted to be; it looked pretty cramped, if I may describe the feather as I would have long ago, when the line between objects and beings had not yet been drawn, and all was alive, and felt, and capable of holding a conversation or being hurt. But, then again, sacred shards of bone, teeth, fingernails, locks of hair have always been made to live in such boxes. I don't think there were colored beads or decorative wraps on the feather (I almost said "on the bird") since a relic, by a kind of mitosis, regenerates spirit, so there exists between part and whole a very fast shimmer that blurs and joins both. What did the feather do in there—rest? Until called upon? What is the life of a sacred thing, beyond waiting to be called forth? Though, too, I believe we are necessary, and that restive powers need to be touched, moved, acknowledged into being. And that the act of enlivening matters.

*

Eagles certainly look ferocious, confident, full of pride: those sharp talons for seizing and beaks for tearing, puffed breasts (though many birds puff up in the cold) and blazing, ever-open eyes (almost human-sized, though four times as sharp). Our country's symbol very much isn't the screech owl, a creature the size of a coffee mug, whose habits include attentive wait-ing, silent diving, erratic flight to confuse its prey, and whose call sounds not at all like a screech, but a distant, whinnying horse. Whose eyes are a buttery yellow, and gently bright. I'd be inclined to choose for an icon a bird who won't much reveal itself, who is shy and alert and requires patience to get to know. Such is the way the best thought comes—over time, very slowly.

Such are the habits of being I'd seek in a national bird—a watchful thing who prefers the edges, who leaves behind a scoured bounty of bones, teeth, and feathers, returned to the earth in neat pellets.

Yes, a screech owl, if I had to go for a singular creature—though it might be better to consider the full expression of our motto, and restore to the epithetic "Out of many, one" the phrase "and one out of all things." We might then have a more capacious illustration of how we actually live together. Consider Lewis Thomas's description of ants, those aggregating minds: "What makes us most uncomfortable is that they . . . seem to live two kinds of lives: they are individuals going about the day's business without much evidence of thought for tomorrow, and they are at the same time component parts, cellular elements, in the huge, writhing, ruminating organism of the Hill, the nest, the hive."

On the coin of *my* realm: heads—a screech owl; tails—a ruminating hive.

*

It's that the eagle is a rock star, and I'm not a fan type. Where crowds gather, I run the other way—toward buzzard, crow, sparrow. The rabble. The common. Definitely the pigeon. Not the brook-voiced mourning dove with its slow grace and musical flight; I mean exactly the city pigeon, oily and bright as a gas station puddle, and not at all bothered by spiked window sills, or ledges sown with shards of glass. Who never hurries, who dodges buses at the very last second, resettling itself in the same perilous spot.

*

My third eagle—an eagle pair, so alike in their fate I can discuss them as one—came a few weeks ago at a small, county zoo in New Jersey. They lived in a well-kept cage enclosed by special, tangle-resistant mesh. At the center was a high platform piled with sticks, the makings of a nest the keepers started, but which, not being mates (pals, yes, they got along fine), the birds wouldn't finish. Eagles don't much like open platforms, and their courtship displays require high, aerial loops, a clasping of talons, a plunge towards earth and quick release. As their keeper said, netting kills the mood. Both were rescued (unintentionally shot, their vision went bad and their wings didn't heal) and couldn't be released into the wild.

Or *what* would happen?

They'd die. Which is, of course, what happens to all birds with lousy sight and bad wings out in the world: they can't hunt well, they bump into things, and turn fast into prey. The longer I looked on—the neat cage with perches and fresh mouse meals—the harder it was to see them as birds, for all the good they'd been done.

*

At the National Eagle Repository, in Commerce City, Colorado, the bodies of dead eagles are collected, cataloged, and frozen.

It's illegal to keep a dead eagle, even if just come upon (say, electrocuted or hit by a truck), so if it's your practice to use eagle feathers in ceremonies, to use talons in dances, or bones, or skulls in prayer, you must first petition the government for the use of any eagle parts.

A bulletin put out by the US Fish and Wildlife Service, Office of Law Enforcement answers questions about the procedures for procuring. "Only enrolled members of Federally recognized tribes can obtain a permit from FWS authorizing them to receive and possess eagle feathers from the Repository for religious purposes." On the application "specify whether you want a golden or bald eagle, a mature or immature bird, a whole bird or specific parts, or have no preference" and "make sure you request either a whole bird or parts. Do not ask for both."

There is also an "approved ceremonies" list, though you're not required to name the religious ceremony if doing so "violates the sanctity of your belief."

Applicants are advised of the long waiting period for birds (for the immature golden eagle, the most in demand, at least five years). There are over five thousand people on the waiting list for the approximately one thousand eagles the repository receives annually. Other wait times include: whole tail only, golden eagle: four to four and a half years; whole tail only, bald eagle: two to two and a half years; pair of eagle wings, approximately one year; trunks, heads, talons only: on receipt of request.

The form is highly specific, so as to carefully dole out birds. "Each applicant can apply for only one whole eagle or specific parts equivalent to one bird (i.e. two wings, one tail, two talons) at a time. *Quality may vary. Applicants may not customize orders."* (The emphasis is theirs.) Since only one order per application is allowed, to obtain feathers to present to students at graduation, "an applicant may reorder and continue to do so throughout the year until the number of feathers needed have [*sic*] been acquired." (Which would make high school graduation planning a year-round task—an undue burden in any court of law.)

That an allotment cannot be customized means take-what-you're-given (as with government cheese), means make-do-with-salvage, or with the ersatz. A site called Real Legal Feathers sells turkey feathers as "a great alternative" and claims "you can wash, dry and preen the web back together just as you would any other natural feather." (Perhaps—and this seems like a reasonable conjecture—if suddenly there was a scarcity of crosses, if crosses were no longer legally available, couldn't one make do with an X? Which is, after all, a sort of cross on its side, a little tipsy and slightly askew, but squint and tilt your head and it's more or less the same thing, no?)

If feathers are earned through deeds, if feathers are the deeds themselves, if eagle trapping sites are sacred and the hunt is undertaken after intense prayer and fasting—and if one must now apply to the government for feathers and parts—how does the sacred proceed? The following-of-directions and checking-of-boxes confers no story, no morning-full-of-anticipation (or weeks, or years), there's no suspension-of-thought-while-tracking, no wind-lifting-eagle and wing-sound-ceasing, the breath of the bird not-gone-but-shifting, the finding-and-entering, the listening-into. . . . If what's as holy as the actual bird is the getting of the bird, if the holy needs for expression a season, death, or occasion, then the filing of forms, and before that even, the freezing, thawing, picking, and packing of eagles recomposes the shape of time.

And made to wait, the holy frays.

*

Of a carved, white wooden bird, an elaborate cutout art practiced in Baltic countries, John Berger writes: "One is looking at a piece of wood that has become a bird. One is looking at a bird that is somehow more than a bird. One is looking at something that has been worked with a mysterious skill and a kind of love." Not so much a symbol of a bird, but an effort "to translate a message received from a real bird." A teasing out of qualities. Not an imitation, but a glimpse, an attempt. As his language, too, is an attempt—each repetition of "one is looking" a return to the beginning, a trying-again, a reconstituting in different angles of light, so that by multiple views one might draw closer to. The bird's not a fixed symbol, but an expression of something hard to catch hold of.

Feathers of wood.

A tree becoming the thing it sheltered; a bird expressing blossoming.

The qualities of one becoming the qualities of the other.

A variation: *In one thing, many.*

*

My fourth eagle was a gathering of birds at the Conowingo Dam, near the spot where the Susquehanna River empties into the Chesapeake Bay. While I didn't see nests, I assume they were there (December is nest-building time for eagles), huge ones, up to thirteen feet deep, and eight feet wide, and weighing more than a ton. That's the size, in my neighborhood, of an average garden shed filled with stuff. I did see more than a dozen eagles, hanging out on rocks in the water, settling in trees, stretching their wings, resting and sunning themselves on transmission towers sunk into the river—not at all the solo creatures I assumed, portrayed as they are in heraldic portraits. (Poland's double-headed eagle always looked like a filleted chicken. And pinioned on the quarter, our eagle's legs are strangely squat, its broad chest pectoraled and unnervingly human. In fact, if you cover its wings with your thumbs, the bird looks like a cartoon prizefighter.)

Unlike black vultures, elegant flyers who coast on thermals, eagles flap a lot and land heavily on bare, sturdy branches. A few times a day at the dam, fish get caught in the turbines and sucked through—so the eagles pluck all they want from the water and hardly have to leave their rocks. They were to me—well, many things. Bigger than I remembered, more wary than the vultures who hunched on low branches and regarded us mildly. Mostly, though, they weren't ferocious, just quietly sunning themselves on that unseasonably warm day. Close up, their beaks were more rounded than hooked, their legs softly feathered, their brows not so heavy—and mussed rather than stern. Maybe because it was so warm, and the breeze so gentle, their eyes seemed a sunny, polleny yellow. With my binoculars, I could see the scales on their talons, some muddy or browned with fish guts, some wet and shining. If I went in closer still, I'd see mites gathered under wing, bits of feather, fungi, and algae. In whatever ways eagles have seemed standoffish—these were not. These stretched and scratched and breathed.

Proximity turns a symbol into a bird again.

*

My final eagle began as an absence, as no eagle at all. Visiting the county dump, where I thought I might see one, turned up instead a lot of hawks. I drove in past the line of cars waiting to deposit household items and parked near the dumpsites, where I got out and looked around. Holding the hawks in my binoculars' lens, I followed them across the very blue sky until they circled higher and turned to dark Vs, backlit by bright sun. The buzzards who tip so gently in wind, swallows skimming the dunes, mockingbirds, grackles, red-winged blackbirds—all moved in and out of sight. It was quiet up on the hill where the bulldozers were parked, and the county keeps pyramids of pipes and old oil drums. I could see the quarry and mulch pit from there, and all around the pear trees in bloom. In the knee-high grass, I surprised a woodchuck who exploded like a brown geyser and ran off fast, its heavy, loose pelt sliding over its back—the word *pelt* as surprising as the animal itself.

There was a peace to the far clanking and grinding, muffled by low, grassy hills, and when the machines stopped for the day, a warm, buzzing stillness rose up again, until the cars started their engines and lined up to leave.

No eagles that day, but now that I've seen more than a few, the thought of one in this summery spot, the thought of it whole and unto itself, made for me a ghost bird. An afterimage. Or a presaging—how can I know what might come to fill this place once I'm gone? A very real bird—here somewhere. Not threatened/ protected, not doled out in parts; not embossed, not marked on a personal checklist. Not derided or rescued. Not burdened with the ideals of a nation. Just yesterday, after reading about two eagles tangled in combat and crashing to earth at an airport in Minnesota, I went out expecting maybe—a sign? There was no eagle on our block that morning (and likely there won't be, here in the city), but instead a sensation, a space in the air in eagle form. It's hard to explain what it felt like—lit, present, ripe—what was that?

Consider the shape of a thought unbound, bound for a moment in the shape of a bird. Then let it mean—not luck, or luck's opposite, not a stranger's arrival, or the promise of riches. To see an eagle, and not a symbol, you'd have to stop wanting the bird to *mean*.

Such an empty, bright, high-domed sky. Put an eagle in it. A scrap, a dot, a spot on sun, smudge in air moving fast out of sight, gone behind trees then back out into light. Give it desires. Its own. What are they? What would an eagle want most from a day?

DOT

I'm a dot. My dog's a white dot. Together we're held in the police helicopter's red searchlight. My dog's a very patient dot—when I stop to think, she sits and waits. I'm remembering: doctor's appointment at two, lightbulbs and milk, and I don't know why, but that woman last week going on and on, giving a bad talk to a bored audience. That she didn't seem to know it was bad. (Embarrassment on behalf of another—a classic dot-trap.) Then, right here in the parking lot: distant laughter; whine of truck brakes slowly slowing like a long, last pull on a fat wine sack; squirrels in dry leaves; hydraulic pops from a building site. Bright, loud civilization-sounds and the pictures they conjure pin a dot down. Hold her in place. There's a figure eight smear in torn-up ground just ahead on a little rise, cut by a Bobcat—an infinity sign, should a dot want a companion. If a dot is open to companions, in they rain: tree-branch arrows pointing the way; fallen, blackened chewing-gum stars.

A dot is a point where life is confirmed. A sign that the parking lot's not a wasteland. (And here comes the copter's red beam again. That faraway eye, looking and looking.) Alone, I don't indicate *teeming* or *throngs* like biotic stuff might: those ever-tempting Sea-Monkeys advertised at the back of comic books, so happy, so lusciously drawn. (What kind of person makes a living by disappointing kids?) Opening a packet, you'd find a spoonful of comma-sized Monkeys; after a few days, they'd fatten up and wiggle around in their jar of warm water. After a week, the Kingdom was a colloidal mess, and not a single Monkey visible. And they never grew those cheery faces. *Lesson learned*, the ad man says, or the illustrator who drew pink, chubby cheeks (and tiara and lashes) to distinguish the princess Sea-Monkey from the guaranteed one-per-pack crowned prince with scepter. Not one developed human-webby feet. "So eager to please they can even be trained!" (Actually, they were eager to eat, so when you tapped in a dose of dusty food, they'd flagella right to it. Even a brine shrimp knows which way is up. When the food ran out—at about the time you were fully sad—the Monkeys were done for.) A dot, though, is not going to disappoint—countable, bodied, roseate if the helicopter's flying at dawn, or as the beam sharpens out of the gloaming against true night, and holds a dot still.

I won't be reviewing dots in pop culture or nostalgically musing on connect-the-dots books, Candy Dots, Dot the nickname—I'm sticking with the original premise: from air, I'm a dot. My dog's a white dot. We're nothing much until brought into focus. And since it's a state-of-the-art police copter, somewhere up there are precision sights—inset in goggles, or dashboard-mounted. A set of crosshairs where I might be centered in lenses so powerful that actual hair (even a nimbus like mine) could be tuned in very finely. The pilot might aim the red beam through my dog's curly tail, which looks like the handle of an old teacup. Or exactly like the tail on a milch cow pitcher. My grandmother's beautiful porcelain one was shaded with brown spots which somehow were rough and suggested real hide. Her cow wore a bronze bell around its neck that tinked when I poured its milk into my cocoa, into everyone's coffee around the table (best little kid job) and made the cow live.

That cow's a dot I hover over—in mind, because my uncle now has it. It isn't gone; it just requires an aerial view. As the past often does. Danger does, too: skulking, milling, suspicious dots a police helicopter doubles back on. Bigger dot too close to smaller? Copter flying lower to check: Big dot throttling smaller dot? Dots in train yards, busting out windows? Single dot running with . . . what? TV? Dot hauling sacks of dot belongings—across tracks, across fields, to dot camp under highway?

At the end of our walk, standing and thinking (my dog's chasing squirrels and out of the scene), I'm so still I might be a splotch of old paint where the lot-lining went wrong. A pile of construction junk. A tangle of branches downed in a storm. But the pilot's trained in dot discernment, in reading shadows and movement so as to reveal a dot's identity—like swinging binoculars up to track birds. Which is way more interesting than birds-at-a-distance.

Just last week, I turned a dot into an eagle. It was hanging out with the other eagles at the head of the Conowingo Dam, pinning a fish to a rock and eating. I could tune in the precise stab and tear, then the pulling of a long, fresh strip of pink. And the way the bird swallowed, head up and gulping, meat in the gullet slowly moving, the bird finished and resting, warmth filling the body, the bird held there, stilled at the center of its day.

For a moment, I'm what the copter's after, what its red eye is tracking. I try to project nonchalant dot behavior. And soon it's clear; I'm not what they want. I'm what the dot they're looking for wants.

I'm a dot's dot. A target, a bullseye.

To a dot on the lam, I'm a *mark*. A *hit*.

For dot spotters, I'm only a *blip*.

Since the cops have lingered overhead, they've reviewed my curious stance, my head inclined, the way just now I bent down to a low rustling, a vole leaving its nearby vole home. They've watched me watch a vole eating something. How it used its long nose and needly claws, and dug and paused and looked around. There's the little trail it made. There's the skirmish mark in dirt where it wrestled with an apple core and took a few successful bites. I'm completely on the up-and-up. Just out vole-spotting. Learning something about vole life.

Steal with your eyes, my grandmother said.

That's what I'm doing.

Though I did not see this elegy coming.

OF PRAYER

It was a quilt of the kind I know to be in most American hotel rooms—synthetic and scratchy on the underside where little pills gather from rubbing, and snags from jewelry make a web of lines. Time marks blankets and towels with thin spots, blinds with frayed slats, toilet seats with chips. Rust stains a sink, and water a nightstand. Quilts of this kind withstand a lot—our antics and rest, much shaking and straightening, rough cleaning—all evidence of the passage of days and nights.

It was early spring, but likely the AC in the room was on. He'd have thought of the sound as *muffling*, a small calculation any mind would make.

Mine would.

I'd think of that.

Maybe he fixed on the single word *muffle* and repeated it a few, then too many times. Any word, under strain, will collapse into garble.

There's a store manager in this, too, you might recognize. Imagine him at the new Crate & Barrel, a few blocks from the hotel. Just hired, proud of his clean and bright unit, a "step lively and much can be yours" kind of guy, with promise and smarts.

Here, when you buy a knife, they wrap it securely in sturdy paper, which indicates they run a safe ship, no bows or gift wrap for the cutlery. They seal such things with a wide strip of tape and let it be your problem undoing it at home. How could he know, the manager-taper, that he had his hands on something terribly wrong? That another hand, one he just touched—showing the balance of hilt and blade, passing the pen to sign the receipt—would act in ways so unthinkable that he himself might feel implicated? Sometimes I touch my dollar bills, especially the fifties, and consider all the bribes they sealed, drugs they scored, and run in my head tests on the microbes, stories, economies I'm passing along in the purchase of onions, sliced turkey, and cheese.

Likely the manager asked a question, a simple one—"Is this a present?" And perhaps his customer said "Yes, it is" very fast, to throw the manager off the trail. And maybe that there *was* a trail, that he himself was still constructing it, became clear for the customer precisely then, and for the first time. It's possible, too, that such a trail might have been shifted by the simplest statement, the way a weatherman might transform a gray morning by saying "a beautiful light rain is falling on the city." Just the other day I was grateful to have my mood shifted once the beauty of rain was suggested. Whole strings of decisions could've been altered, the more instructions a chatty manager gave at the register, if he was good at building relations—as in "be careful with this, it's wrapped well for now, but if you intend to post it or gift it . . ." (The verbing alone might have startled the buyer: How weird: *to gift!* How archaic: to *post!* And "to wash this knife . . ." alone might have done it.) The more time shared at the register, where one man was working the hip/bright store, and the other planning the murder of his family, the more some internal diffusion of light, a breaking of clouds, a breakthrough, a breakdown, a falling-to-knees-and-trembling sort of scene, a right and good rending in the name of healing, like breaking to reset a bone— might have halted things. I'd like to believe that more chat, the right words, the weight of them, would've shoved a wedge in and filled the hole in the air before him—emptiness in the chest, rent in the logic—where instead more unthinkable acts firmed up.

It's a quilt with a busy gray and brown pattern, dark-toned to hide stains you very much don't want to think of—from, say, couples not-waiting and tearing into each other, spilled drinks, muddy shoes.

The quilt, rolled and kicked. Bunched on the floor. Dampened. Stepped on.

Trampled, balled, twisted.

That quilt.

There it was. That's what I saw on this brisk, fall day. It came unbidden, the way so many things, as I'm walking, come in—on stippled light (or gray light, or very bright sun), landing and piercing.

In its place, I tried to install quilts *I've* made. Three altogether. One for a boy who cared nothing about quilts, which my mother watched me make as I listened over and over to *Jesus Christ Superstar* for weeks one summer. Fervently, I'd say, singing into the belief of others but not, myself, possessing anything like their strain of it. The second one was for a friend who appreciated it greatly and who gave more to me than I could accept at the time. And the last I made for myself. I still have it, pieced mostly from little-kid dresses, kerchiefs, and smocks my mother made. I recall with ease, by way of these colors (summer-sky, corn-yellow), an old atmosphere: deep snowy mornings when I'd stand on a chair and look out the kitchen window a long while. The trees at the front of the house were just planted, and because I was young, too, we understood each other. The quiet hummed. It was before the world was up, my box turtle crawled around in his tank, and the far-off flagpole in the park was a very dark gray against the brighter, snow-packed sky. I came to understand distance then, by feeling the plot of a day hovering and the space where I stood, a central point. By being still, I could collect what the day was trying to say.

Thus, I let the ruined quilt come in.

I locate the pockets and dips, deep valleys for terrible pools and rivers; in patterns, streams swell, spill, and seep. I let the puddles turn rusty in air.

To be in the business of letting the blood come.

We each have our fields. The word *field* is capacious—a place to be turned, planted, gathered from. Field of light, of inquiry, of—and here I'm getting closer—*battle*. One man's, with his soul, and he lost very completely.

Explanations fail.

Plenty don't murder who you'd expect might.

A man with no hope acts like a knife. Failed financial schemes act like a knife. A sham is a knife. Shame is a knife. Fear, a knife that cuts a caul of darkness out and hangs it over all of us, like— once I saw in a restorer's hands—a sheet of gold leaf lifted on the edge of a blade, struck up like a flame, and laid over the hem of a wooden saint, then rubbed to a shine. But this knife held no light at all. Knife like a drowning. Quilt like a vessel, mop, body bag, grave. Snarled. Fretted. Bogged. Consigned and corrupted. He'd brought his wife and younger daughter to visit the older daughter at college. She went that afternoon to the hotel, and when it got late and she hadn't returned, her roommates called. Her father answered and said not to worry, she was going to spend the night with the family. At which point, he'd already killed them all. Soon after that, he turned the knife on himself.

The girl went to the university where I teach. She was, as I learned, much loved by her friends. She was kind and had plans, exams, parties upcoming.

A bed. A wardrobe. Pencils. Soap. Socks.

The day after the tragedy, when the story broke, we heard the breaking. Hearing it made the sun incongruous. Made me try to say something into the warmth it kept giving—poor sun, always shining on everyone, brightening all events in its path. In one of my very best classes (where soon, at the end of the semester, one student was heading to China, one into the army, one to teach at a city school) what I said about the tragedy wasn't *nothing*—it was just the best I could do. Given my limits. Since I hadn't a practice. Which was better than nothing, but still weighed very little. I said something like: Though you might not have known her, she was part of your day. A presence you passed as you crossed the quad, a laugh you heard and took in, and in that way, she colored your stubborn loneliness. She brushed crumbs off the table before you sat down. She exhaled as she passed and air held the breath you drew into your body. You caught her cold. You swallowed her sigh. You picked up the penny she dropped, thinking "hey, lucky penny." And just as she gave proof to your day, you gave hers shape, maybe lit her afternoon with your colors, voice, presence.

The quilt reddened. The quilt twisted and fell. The funerals were separate, the girls with their mother, the father apart, and, yes, people did attend his. How would he feel, I remember thinking, floating above his body (where, for the sake of this thought, I put him) seeing what the mourners made, best they could, of the wreckage he caused. How they forced the persistence of some goodness to live. Made themselves hold opposing forces, admit there was good, there had been in him, and allowed that mystery to compel them to come. Or they were obliged because family, and that's what you do.

All loss is weighted with disbelief. All homage seeks to make something to keep, to make loss mean, to give the fissile core of grief shape. The quilt bore the weight of the act, of the bodies; and since such fabric isn't absorbent, it must've made *channels*, and there the blood pooled. There were *runnels*. And *chambers*.

Words very like *muffling* kept coming: fleet, shocking, precise, and unspoken.

When I suggested we take a moment of silence, each one of

them, every single student, bowed and prayed. What rattled me, though of course it shouldn't have (this being a Catholic university), was that they had a prayer ready and knew what to say, while I had to make something up on the spot about breath and pennies and each of us being assumed into another's day.

And what *did* they say?

I asked a few of them this fall, now a year and a half later, if they remembered that moment and what they were thinking. One said she created a silence around herself and asked, she didn't know who, the force she was used to calling "God," for comfort and healing on the family's behalf. Another with no go-to prayer either recalled the sensation of bowing her head with everyone. I told her I feared that I, alone, had no prayer. She said she'd always suspected we bow our heads to hide our faces, to keep from each other how ashamed we feel in the face of grief. For another, the Prayer for the Faithful Departed came first, and then a rush of fear: My father was also out of work then, she said, and things were bad. If no one in *her* family saw it coming . . . what kept *us* from being *them*? The last one I asked—I think of him as especially adept at matters of the spirit—didn't recall what he thought or prayed. But he said that after her death (they were friends) nothing was the same. One day he was a kid, working, hanging out, and the next, everything changed. And when another classmate died soon after, and he found himself repeating the steps—go to the Mass, go to the grave—that shook him: the familiarity. After that, he no longer wondered how adults always seemed to know what to do.

Why does she come back now, in fall?

I'm on the same path I take every day. I had no intention of recalling her—but stories lay themselves over the land. Leaves-losing-color, then trees-losing-leaves—that's an old one: Demeter's loss of Persephone.

Any land looks like death when the blooming's done and nothing's green for months on end.

One naturally mourns a girl in fall—though I have no fixed date for calling her back. Nothing like All Souls' Day, when, ten years ago now, my own friend jumped to her death. It was a bitter October in Warsaw, and climbing the stairs to the top of the building, sensible as she was, she probably wore her big coat. *Why*, though? Why, at the end, bother? And the heavy door to the roof—why wasn't it locked? (Though we used to go up there all the time, the city sky finally vast in the dark, the tram a bright river, the apartment blocks like hunched, far-off mountains if you squinted and undid the chimneys.) Was there a moment the wind calmed and she paused, looked at her shoes, thought *Those are my shoes and I laced them this morning*?

Every year since, each thirty-first of October, a new piece of that scene fills in, makes a bid for inclusion. As if remembering better might bring some ease, and precision upend disbelief. Once it was the single step up to the building's edge. Another time, that old twig broom and dented ash can. In other years, lines of tar sealing cracks in the roof; a silver bucket with frozen washrags; the wobbly handrail; the switch plate's stiff toggle on the wall at the foot of the stairwell.

One year, no scene formed (that was a dark time) and the cold itself had to suffice.

This year it was a scent that came—the hallway's mix of cigarette smoke, stew meat, wet boots, and coal. When the smell dissipated, the actual things—cigarettes, boots, and black dust over everything—remained. Insisted. Asserted. Oh strange and constant spring.

IN THE DESPOILED
AND RADIANT NOW

after a line by Stephen Dunn

A group of us had gathered on the porch for a drink at the end
of the day—late August, Vermont, sun bright-but-downshifting,
leaves green-but-red-tinging—when a moose wandered into the
meadow behind the house. She stood chest-deep in the tall grass,
so dark she shone like a black, still lake. No one had ever seen a
moose in that spot, or so close. Just an hour earlier, I was circling
the mowed edge of the meadow, woods on one side, milkweed on
the other; with my arms outstretched I could almost touch both.
As I walked—and there isn't a *why* to be had in this story—I
was conjuring *moose*. Considering it a moose-like day, and why
wouldn't one want to step out of the woods—not to see me but
just because. Because if I were a moose, I'd want exactly, full and
straight on, summer turning, the air sweet, the greens thick. Then
the moment cracked open, stretched wide, went deep, and it was
moose all around. My own measure was moose-hipbone-high;
each hummock I stepped on was spanned by a hoof, each branch
overhanging muzzled out of the way. A musky, rich, rooty scent
rose and a hunger drew powerfully forth (those catkins so tender
I wanted a mouthful). I don't know why it wasn't a deer, hawk,

or fox moment; I have no experience at all with moose-presence. But that's what came.

And then—there she was. Golden where sun touched her haunches. Wet-nosed, mouth full, and quivering at flies, before a porch full of noisy observers.

I don't mean to centralize myself in this story—just that I had been in a state to sense moose, and was given to register ease, ripeness, desire in a way not my own. When the moose turned after maybe ten minutes of chewing and watching, and shuffled back to the woods in her heavy, mild way, everyone on the porch applauded.

But I kept what happened earlier to myself. Telling would've made it a footnote, or worse, a groovy synchronicity. That such a moment marked *me* wasn't a point I wanted to make. What it did mean, though, is such things can be trusted, such moments held and believed. Like yesterday's fast certainty that the street I live on, the ground below, was suffocating, and all the arterials, rivulets, creek beds, all the would-be nest sites, spots where seeds might have rooted and greened, while not dead, were only partly alive. The chart I consulted on how roads are made, the multiple layers for weight-bearing and drainage, the fixed order and variety of materials poured and packed in confirmed it: no simple, cartoonish peeling away, no rolling up of asphalt like a rug would be possible. And suddenly seeing the road—no, *hearing* its straining, a sharp in-suck—that was an unbidden grief on a otherwise beautiful fall afternoon.

A body's desire for sun-on-flank, and the land's stoppered

breath in search of release. An unseen moose making herself felt, and stifled land registering in the chest—such moments arrive trailing their shine, flagging their ruin. Without words they come calling and let their rogue impression be held. That taste in the air of musk and hunger, the feel of a street's very hardened skin—such is my latest proof: there exist ways of listening a listener hardly understands. In the despoiled and radiant now, these moments approach—the presence of ease and the presence of ruin, a lit stillness, a dense grief, impossible to unknow—like any great love or loss taken into the body.

ALL THE FIERCE TETHERS

The general pattern, its motions within itself lithe-unfolded, slow, gradual, grand . . . —JAMES AGEE

I used to think *how sad*, maybe even *how pathetic*, our small lives, so many lives in houses or apartments, with children or not, each morning everyone putting on clothes, working their jobs, buying their food. That everyone loved their days, or didn't and kept on anyway seemed a trick, an ambush—a newsreel might have called it the "promise of progress," when really such living looped like a trolley circling a town, the tracks slick with wear. Even before any real sense of daily routine kicked into motion, most forms of habit felt like a trap. *Everyone's life precious to them* seemed to me a sort of defeat, a placation, the phrase itself a patronizing pat on the head.

Yet a day unhitched from the orderly currents of morning, noon, evening—how makeshift and slight that, too, would be.

In place of accepting a conventional day, or making one up on my very own terms, what did I want? Meaning imparted from somewhere on high, say a steep, backlit cliff with a windy voice that led to an edge where I'd stand and face off with the queasiness?

All those lives, self-powered, like emergency generators—I

couldn't imagine the vast number of them—or rather, I could imagine too well. I got the gist, I'd traveled and learned the variations, took on new habits as needed—in Warsaw, All Souls' Day picnics in freezing graveyards with vodka and blood sausages; in Moscow, the rubles folded and slipped into documents at the border. But those variations only proved my point, returned me to the initial sensation: that the loop, circuit, routine was everywhere pulsing along, ongoing, unending, then ending.

I should say, too, the looping sensation was more a set of suspicions, a nagging or twinge, than an articulated fear, and that it broke through only briefly, but sharply, like a headache after an icy drink. It's nearly impossible to conjure up now for more than a second the circumstances leading to this particular displacement. What I've gathered up here sounds harsher than I mean to convey, for my life at the time wasn't harsh-feeling as much as wobbly, the contours uncertain, the hours either baggy and irregular, or taut with desire.

All this returned recently when, stopped at an intersection, I saw a woman leaving a dentist's office en route to her car. She dug around in her bag and pulled out her keys. *She'll head home, park, switch on a light as she enters the hallway*, I thought. The rattling keys, a hall light switched on—that's all it took. Just knowing that she (like anyone) moved through a day with practiced gestures (washing dishes, snapping sheets just out of a dryer—or letting everything encrust or wrinkle) led to the old onrush of a world full of others' inscrutable days unfurling right there on the street—all the tea-wallahs filling glasses on trays, somewhere the bite of warm camel milk, hickory wood falling in curls from a carpenter's plane in Vermont, markets in Istanbul, bighorn sheep, manta rays, cities, doomed glaciers—every hidden or known subject under study, or in ruins, all vastly worthy, and there, alongside the rush of human endeavors and moments, my own glancing portion. My own brief day.

Now when I watch people (through binoculars, as is my habit when I look up from my work and need a break) it's exactly the boundedness of their lives, the precise sizing down that moves me. How absorbed and unprotected they are. Lavishing attention comes easily then: across a few backyards and a street, there's the deep drag he takes on his cigarette, how he flicks the ash deftly (a lifelong smoker), scratches his ear, and draws down the last bit. Stubs the butt in the flowerpot. Hikes his pants up. Opens the door and stops for a final look at the frame, which, running his thumb along, he confirms needs fixing (sanding, from the way he's plucking the wood), a job I imagine he adds to the list-in-the-head . . . and then the door closes on my tableau, compact enough to slip into a pocket—though there's always more to be had, swing the lenses in any direction: garbage man spitting into the truck, wandering dog sniffing just-planted tree. Binoculars make my subjects palm-sized, full of intention, and set in motion by an ordering force.

Then, of course, there are my own small moments, fixed in their own tondos of light, all the common stuff touched in the course of a day—each door's glass knob, cool even in summer;

my grandmother's wooden spoons worn smooth as bone by decades of stirring. My people, my loves. All the fierce tethers to all the fierce moments—they matter, to the pinpoint I've become. That's the dizzying thing—how the vastness of my singular life does not set me faceless in the ranks of billions, except that it does. I am perfectly speck-like. My days resemble the days of others. That a small portion no longer roils with puniness but is measured in units of transience, and that I take up my day, my sliver, despite—that's fearsome.

About the phrase "In the beginning, God created heaven and earth," a friend writes, "Depending on a subtle difference in pronunciation, signaling the presence or absence of the definite article, the construct could be different: *be*'resheet instead of *ba*'resheet—not 'in *the* beginning' but 'in *a* beginning' God created . . ."

Imagine each event or being tethered to its originating breath, each moment momentous unto itself, each microflash hot with insistence, finding the contours it alone wants. Surrounded with time, given its space and its very own immanence (the darkness over the face of the deep, gradations of morning pinking up), each beginning is equal in its drive to exist. As John Donne preached in his Sermon XXI in 1628, "All things that are, are equally removed from being nothing." Thus, everything composed apart from absence, all creatures by way of simply existing, stand shoulder to shoulder in the eyes of the present. Or for Barbara McClintock, who so loved from the start of her work on

DNA the many shapes of the smallest minds in all their manifestations, whose affection measured not parts *to* wholes, divided and dutiful in their contributions, but parts *as* wholes ("Every component of the organism is as much of an organism as every other part"), her feeling for the smallest functioning elements not a fussiness but a scope.

All systems have their principles, their signature handholds, paths for speeding or tarrying along, lines to speak, procedures to follow, and when in good order, the invitation of one is answered by another. The reliance of one upon its partners isn't a leaning-on due to weakness, but a cache of singular minds, territories, instincts maintaining a whole, and so well convened they appear to be one. From every angle and everywhere. As when in the warm waters of the South Pacific, the giant clam (up to four feet across and weighing as much as five hundred pounds) and the algae, zooxanthellae, make together an extravagance of efficiency, a concision of means. Open to light, reddening on the lip of the clam, the zooxanthellae take in sun, thresh it, and offer a harvest of sugars and protein to their host (though *host* isn't right—since one isn't homebound and the other visiting), while in return (or not *in return* but more *as operations go*) the clam protects the delicate algae, locks the gates, darkens the field in the presence of predators.

Or consider the work of carpenter bees, their holes as exact as those made by a drill, that rote machine whose effect we call *perfect*. The holes we have here on our new back porch, bitten bright and still ragged, were made overnight by patient chewing.

The wood's unseasoned, new-grass green, and so young I could press a fingernail in, or leave tooth marks of my own, which, meant for no purpose, wouldn't be in the least bit beautiful. Like any unselfconscious creation, these holes bear the mark of a maker upon them, an order and balance, their edges dusted with neat, rolled specks which soon, all the soft-bellied entries and exits will burnish entirely away. A few inches in, the path takes a sharp right turn and there the queen builds separate chambers for her young and stocks each pantry with a fat ball of pollen. The holes are precisely centered in each beam, not too close to an edge or joist. How uniformly cool it must be in those rooms. How well the young sleep and grow strong in dark, cool, quiet conditions—at least that's been my experience.

I saw a video recently about a guy who casts ant colony "sculptures" by pouring molten aluminum into their nests. As the long tongue of hot metal is tipped from a bucket into the hole, the mound darkens, steams, and sinks a little under the searing, and all the roads and tunnels fill up. When everything cools and hardens he digs the nest out, scrapes off the ash and dirt, and sprays it all clean with a hose. The nests are up to two feet in length and branch off like any living system designed to circulate life, whose handiwork serves a greater good. Highways and storage rooms, fungi farms, livestock aphids, nurseries, resting spots for tired workers, loom studios (none of this is fanciful, I've used not a single metaphor here)—all incinerated. He sells the Vesuvian sculptures for hundreds of dollars (all inquiries must be made privately). "Intricate!" "Amazing!" say his satisfied customers. (One comment reads: "I run a home daycare and we are currently doing a unit on ants. Your video . . . is great for a visual while explaining ant 'cities' to the children. They thought it was so cool they want to watch it again and again. A three-year-old did ask me what happened to the ants. I told him they packed up and moved away!")

If the word *sculpture* here requires even a little dissembling, and the appreciation of form a severing of means from ends, I imagine one would begin with the usual tactics, and from a lordly position: *Ants are the most plentiful species on earth,* or more simply still: *They're only ants. And fire ants at that.* Whom no one likes. (Yes, *whom*—not *which*, not *things*—and to push further still, let's call the grammatical case *the direct indispensable* to help snap ant lives back into focus, or, according to the rules of grammar, into the subject position.)

It's a minor corrective, I know. Fussy-sounding and secondary to concerns about swarming and stinging, which centralize us. Though left to their work, fire ants will aerate miles of soil, control boll weevils, corn worms, and sugarcane borers, eat fleas, ticks, termites, mosquitoes, and scorpions.

If beauty's understood as a form of order, its elements perfectly self-regulating, then an orderly day is not a worn circuit, or rote, but a haven and a habitat. And the work of those matched to their tasks, shifting as one, like flocks in a thermal or schools in a river, like beings dedicated to wind, hunger, scent, laws entirely their own—that work, if beheld, fires into awe—a sudden erasure of self, an internal, unbidden stillness.

Now though, more and more, the most basic systems are

identified first by way of their ruin. One comes to know them only briefly in their magnificence, before news of their loss takes up its platform, then overtakes the conversation—and rightly, since the conversation is finally urgent.

The snowshoe hare, brimming with muscle, and cunning, and flight, once lived emplaced in an elegant system.

Stay with me now. I'll slow it way down.

We're in Glacier National Park in Montana. As soon as the days begin to shorten, the hare's meadow-brown fur, triggered by changes in the length of daylight, begins to whiten. Linger exactly here, in this moment, so the present won't grow suddenly steep, break off, and slide under. It's autumn. A hare's exchanging one coat for another, brightening as the afternoon dims. The hare's moving like snow, its back is a soft, blowing drift as it runs. When still, the hare is a snow-covered rock, white fur prickling like early frost.

Now having been with, having seen even briefly, knowing something of the hare in its rightness, we can shift.

As we must, so we can go on.

As a result of rising temperatures, the snows are coming much later these days and the hare, leashed to the light's firm hand, is exposed too soon, its whiteness loud, a wrong dialect in a hostile town making it vulnerable and thus, overhunted—a situation that affects the lynx as well, whose primary prey is the hare. Pushed to move to higher ground but without new corridors for migration (the land too dense with fast-growing pines, which easily adapt to warmth) the lynx are vanishing, too.

And so, on it goes.

This isn't news to those who study the behaviors of hare and lynx, or the lives of meadows and languages of trees, but hearing about it for the first time?—how quickly a vast and functioning system is summed up. The once-perfect latitudes, seasons, and cycles, the animal tasks and animal knowing—I had to work hard to compass the interdependencies, take in all the microlinks in the food chain. *Food chain*: what an ugly phrase, one that hardly expresses the sensitivities involved, the stalking and crouching and held breath all around, *chain* showing none of the fine calibrations of hares taken down in rightful ways, weakened by age or cleanly startled—or, hares *not* giving up but deftly escaping, the balances of luck, stamina, circumstance, the whole range of live possibilities that make up the health of a system abiding.

And in this way, too, *nest* hardly speaks to the scope of ant cities, ant wainwrights and coopers, nannies and farmers, and (stay for a moment underground now) neither do *roots* reveal the conversations of meadows, the plans worked out for distributing water, the rhizomatics by which needs are met and decisions made in times of want. And *fire* (whose heart is regenerative, whose scorching releases seeds buried deep in the vaults of cones) looks merely destructive unless cycles are tracked in their proper time and from the distance of centuries.

How late we are in coming to full-on views of once-perfect systems, arrangements now so chafed by ruin they're barely readable anymore. How to hold them—quickly, I mean, we can't linger too long, there's much work to do—when cascades of fresh bad news daily overrun their brilliance.

It's work to hold, to come to love the parts and particulars of a meadow, nest, day. Slow work. Investment—not "money down" but the older form, "the act of dressing to encounter the holy." It's work to track a field of white moving up a hare's back—and to see, in turn, how the lengthening dark lends to snow its animal form. Work to still the parts of a day, to keep the parts close as they welter and dim. Are overcast or siphoned away. Work to call order back into sight, even as it's root-cut, or blown. Dismantled. Confounded. Torn.

To understand ruin, know first what it is that's being ruined. And here it's exactly the minutiae that matter: piles of washed and folded sheets, neat stacks of ant-cut twigs. Stay with them. All the balances and adaptations that urge themselves forth or retract in disguise, or swarm, or concentrate. That make up a day. Sheering and shorn, burnt and cinched-in—but not wholly gone. Those delicacies. Those radiant systems. Hold them.

THREE-LEGGED BRANCH

First came the sudden, light-struck feel of entering a meadow, though I was deep in the woods in Maine. The pines were thick, the green was black, the sun came only in spots through leaves, so the branch shining up in a little clearing caught and kindled who knows how. But there it was, leaning back, unabashed; stripped and smooth—a small branch with three legs and an ass wrenched around front.

There it was, propped in a split, two delicate legs off to the right, the left one longer and sturdier. At the center, that little crack—tender meridian of a peach, runnel in dirt fresh-cut by rain. Where the legs end and the feet would be are patches of bark like cuffed jeans. (I keep the branch right here on my sill.) One foot touches lightly down, tentative but charged and alert, like a divining rod drawing up the news from far in.

Those rightful three legs.

And what about them conjured the rightness?

The branch holds itself up as a body does, as I do in bed in the morning on elbows, facing the early light. That the curves of the ass move together so gently, then rise and break off where a waist would be, ought to disturb. And the footless legs. The defense-lessness. The whole unprotected against stares and double-takes.

Ought to disturb but doesn't. Why? Finding it there in the woods, that moment unfolded in time not-mine-alone. Offering/beckoning, both came at once. It wasn't event, but en route and steep, like that spot at the edge of a cliff where you—wait.

If I tilt the branch up, the two-legged side poses the way I sometimes stand, one leg crossed over the other. I know how this looks—impatient, unstable, but try it: how good it feels to fight with discomfort for steadiness.

In the woods that morning, what steadied me? That I got offered a way to see—not in-spite-of-the-weirdness, or make-the-best-of-this-oddness, but the twisted body, its three-legged-ness just unto itself. The ass in front, wrong-though-not. Not at all. More that the branch refuses wrongness, drains it away. And that it came this summer when so much else failed, when I didn't know how to hold anything, and my life was burning. That I was moved to pick the branch up. Saw and reached down. Held and knew fast—not with the speed of efficiency, but an unequivocal snap-went-the-knowing.

Let me abide it, so sure in my body.

Abide what? Not the compensatory holiness of the cripple, endowed with spirit as consolation, given the keys to some far-off kingdom in exchange for whole limbs, and ever serving as a sign to us all—cue to be grateful, praise our strong bodies—not that shit. It's the parts cohering as they will, in their way, throwing wide an embrace. No spectacle here, just invitation, ongoing. A thing come upon offered a way to see and be with.

And I saw and was with. We, each, were the site-of.

*

Once I *believed*—though *believed* isn't right. I, child-wise, knew the not-indifference. I was given no church, no practice, no prayer (no under-the-breath rote anything to lean on) so it happened with color, with tide pools, with trees—which called me to them, and in their sight, I was heard, a see-hearing, a searing. Later, that this was *naïve* I surely picked up on, a proto-stance I was meant to exchange for more advanced versions I did not want and do not want now, wherein nothing speaks but in givens and tropes.

All things want to speak in their voices.

As when I visit the ruined oak near my house, and put my hands on its splintered body, move close and slip in (you can too, conversation seeks bodies). The tree here-but-thinned, because split in a storm. Land-stranded, root-torn. Still gathering light. And the listening-in? I never did shed it. It did not get lost. It just rested in me. It was restless in me.

And now is not resting.

METAPHOR STUDIES

SKINNED MUSKRAT

The story on the radio is being reported in a very particular key: New York bemused. If you've grown up with this, it just sounds like fact: how quirky and unfathomable are the provinces! For an instant though, the tone shifts and feels more expansive— like muskrat skinning might be something more. Could stand for *ambition* and translate into *values* we all understand: set a challenge, work hard, move up in the ranks. Listening for that note checks smirkiness, quiets a certain form of laughter at the down-home thangs people do. And if that's the way the listening goes, if things get even briefly metaphorical, then we get to be Rhonda, who won this year's contest. She's us at our best. A version of diligence. Someone who thinks at night to herself how she might make improvements, at a stoplight considers adjustments of tools, the best ordering of gestures. Runs replays. Feels, even as she cuts an apple, the musculature's joy in its training, or when undressing a very muddy child, how adept she's become at improvising around slippery problems. You can hear the moment the reporter slows. Deepens her question. Depatronizes. Gives Rhonda a chance to speak. Gets, actually, interested.

Hearing *that* feels like turning a corner and catching a breeze on an otherwise stifling street.

LANDFILL AND BODIES

A gash hurts, bleeds, scabs over, and in time mends, as grass comes to a torn and bare place, grows over a landfill so you can say of it *hill*, or *far rise*.

Lay the words on a scale: on one side the body, on the other, land. Let *city dump* mean *your cut arm*. Let *greened* be *your skin made whole*.

What once was ruined land might be reclaimed.

To have a doctor who'd say it like this—*Your body will be a field again*.

As will Fresh Kills in Staten Island, NY ("kills" from the Dutch for *stream*, *brook*, or *channel*), a stretch of land three times the size of Central Park. At its peak as a dump, Fresh Kills received twenty-nine thousand tons of garbage a day, from all five boroughs. The stench was so bad that passing it en route to the city, you had to breathe into a handkerchief. Gulls roved in clouds that darkened the sky. Rats had their kingdom. The highest mound was eye to eye with the Statue of Liberty.

In 2001, two million tons of wreckage from 9/11 was trucked to Fresh Kills for sorting.

For months, Fresh Kills was an open grave (the name wasn't lost on anyone). More than three hundred people were identified from the remains.

And though it's been closed for over ten years, the marsh

grasses and miles of soft green still surprise—in the way, long after recovery, getting up from a chair and running to answer a knock at the door—no wincing, no forethought—still feels miraculous.

If "humor is tragedy plus time," a ruin plus time can be sanctuary. In thirty more years, according to plan, Fresh Kills will include a seed farm, nursery, bird refuge, a field full of turbines and a green space memorial where people can stroll, picnic, remember.

A dump restored is a body healed.

A scar is a plaque on the body's field.

Body of land, *leg* of a journey—see, all along you've been in training.

SPRING

Almost ten years ago this spring, I was desperate about many things, but my grandmother was still alive. It was hard to see frothy dogwood blossoms, to pass a magnolia's tender pink cream or the fresh tips of evergreens touched by wind. Everything hurt. Now I breathe freely, move through currents of rough scent rising—mud, cut grass, some wild bloom swelling, releasing a milky sweatiness. I'm washed in waves of sidewalk heat. Shade in bowers, tides of noise—all *here*, and I'm alongside. But my grandmother is gone.

What is *that*?

A Möbius strip.

PRAYER

On my way home after a very long day, I have to decide: Should I walk in the street, or along the reservoir at the top of the hill?

Street: I get to see used condoms, crack baggies, broken spar-kles of windshield glass—basic, shining, urban grit I use to put together stories. Up the hill I get an expanse of clear water and air sweetened by the breath of plants at the banks. Today, *up* sounds best, like what I need most. Spirit is located *up above*, no? So I might rise above my worries and in that way lift my heart?

Though the reservoir is fenced. Another security camera was just installed (post-9/11 concerns) and a maintenance crew is loudly mowing.

Metaphors get compromised. Get eroded and need updating. Rerouting. Reconstituting.

SURPRISE

From a stump, green shoots grow. How tiring to see that and think, *Ah, Spring!* Or a single tulip blooms before all the others in the largest bed in the park—and what's that, *bravery?* And skipping ahead, late August: goldfinch-on-a-spent-sunflower as *harbinger of fall?* Drops of fresh blood on the sidewalk (how fatly they pool before drying out)—what would that be: *the life force ebbing?*

Stop, known equivalencies!

I want my spring flowers unassigned. Bare. To fly past rebirth. I want green to finger the throat of air. Let stumps not *sprout*, but *harbor* and *castle*, be brainpans for a hive of thought, stirred awake, hungry, open-mouthed, gaping.

Shining cat on the neighbor's roof: *black nest of sun*.

Everything always just come upon.

SUBWAY

Seeing a guy on the subway one morning (notable for his pur-
ple-and-yellow striped slicker and red-fringed umbrella), and
then later that day, on a different line, there he is again. That
means, if I let it mean. Suggests the workings of fate uncharted,
all the meetings that go unnoticed. Falling cartoon anvils that
missed me. Occasions for gratitude, overlooked. Occasions for
fear I'm not given to see.

There he goes, up the stairs and away.

To be for someone a metaphor is to be not yourself but a measure of things, the site where chance firms and vastness bright-
ens—you, trying to get home after a long day at work, in your
heavy raincoat and couture umbrella, your throat sore and head
hurting. You who are tired and just want to lie down.

AUTOMATON

Seated at his little desk, this one was built to sketch a ship. He's
geared to hold a long brass pen engraved with twining fleur-de-
lis. The boy with pink porcelain cheeks and a swipe of brown
hair pauses and tilts his face up as if conjuring the next perfect
mast-and-rigging, before turning back to his paper to draw it.
He adds curled waves and puffs of clouds. I can hear the cogs at
work on a flag, a sail, an expanse of deck—the shush of a thought
turning over, a quiet click in the neck as he nods, his left hand
caressing a thought-shape in air. So that what I feel is—and
here, I can't peel back the skin of it very easily. The sensation
pushes past vanity (how Romantic a person looks when writing),

past the uncanny (shiver of the inanimate made flesh)—and into weird certainty: *I know what he's feeling*—ache in the shoulder from sitting too long, internal cams controlling the pen strokes, the eye blinks, the thought-pause. The distinction so quick—not I'm *like* but I *am*.

OPTICAL ILLUSION

I've always liked that image where a young woman in a fur stole, looking over her shoulder, shifts (when you refocus from black space to white) to reveal an old woman with a pointy, hooked nose. I like that little shudder, the way each contains the other, the easy slippage from delicate necklace to tight-lipped grimace. But then, when I saw it the other day, this refinement came: to really get what the picture's suggesting, I'd have to look in a mirror and be shocked. I'd have to feel age as a scrim, or a veil over my present face—and I don't feel that yet. I still look like what I know myself to be. I understand the illusion, but not intimately.

Some metaphors one has to grow into.

FRISBEE

The red disc gets stuck in a tree—it's a blustery day but the thing's held fast, like an apple on a tough stem. We wait for the wind to blow it out (which would make the Frisbee a windfall fruit) but when a gust comes, it just lifts and adjusts. Then a bigger gust comes and the Frisbee falls. And there it is: a way to understand being subject to forces I can't resist. I watch and feel what *buffeted* is: my heart pushed around on a bright fall day.

CHILDREN IN THE BACKGROUND

In the still-dark morning sky, the moon's a white water stain. Then it's a lozenge dissolved by noon. Then at night it takes on a face. It looks upon us.

A face has its dark side. Joy waxes and wanes.

Tides of excitement can overcome a child at a birthday party.

Say a father's away at war; he might as well be in another galaxy, in his tank, on Skype as the cake is cut. A child could say *My father is a star. My father is sand.* And she'd be right in so many ways.

*

Sometimes when we saw the war on TV—and the villages burned, and the people ran—the picture would dissolve. We said *it turned to snow*, it was winter after all, it was very hot in Vietnam but all the kids still turned to snow, they were that far away and that close.

*

One afternoon, I hovered a finger over a pill bug, touched it gently and watched it roll up. I did that a few times, then curled up next to it. My mother came out and said, "Are you hurt?" "No, I'm a pill bug." By which I meant, *I don't want to be seen.* I'm gray. A pebble. A pinfeather. *Safe.*

PLATE GLASS WINDOW

A pebble. A pinfeather. A broken-necked sparrow on sparrow-brown stones. The moss green, the gaps dark, the peace in between. River stones as smooth as eggs. A finger in moss for the velvety damp. Ruffle of feathers the weight of an eyelash. My hard-bent wrist doing angle-of-broken. Try, with your body: *I'm that*, or *That's me*. The order won't matter, one thing is another—neither's only itself, but spreads across continents, yards, galaxies. Species.

To alter one thing is to alter another.

LOON

To alter one thing is to alter another.

If a metaphor is an ecosystem, a way of revealing unseen dependencies, *You're a loon* as a way to say *crazy* isn't so simple anymore. Loons who eat fish full of mercury and breathe air contaminated by coal-fired plants can't incubate properly. Their eggs thin or don't hatch. And mercury wrecks the nervous system. The loons don't act right; they're not loon-like but uncoordinated, nervous, exhausted. Their feathers fledge unevenly, so flying is harder, migration's thrown off, and they can't maintain breeding territory.

Mad as a hatter in centuries past referred to the dementia caused by mercury used in making felt hats. (*To hatter* means also *to weary, to wear out with fatigue*.) Milliners suffered loon-like symptoms, all the confusions and disturbances, plus tremors, sweating, loss of hair, teeth, and nails.

If you want to reflect the moment's concerns, language can't mean in ways it used to. *You're a loon* might still indicate *crazy* as expressed by the bird's ghosted, shuddery call—but *crazy* complicates and layers up. Poison alters etymology's DNA. If a loon's driven mad by poison, if it cannot mate, and cannot care—for its young or about its fate—you'll have to recognize *that* in its call. And if you can hear that, imagine the sound you'd make on a late summer night, at a cool, blue, Adirondack lake—you there with your mate, with no way of increasing yourself, or yourselves, as a pair. And how desperate you'd sound, in your grief.

UNABASHED, WITH RIVER

Try saying, *The earth is my mother.* Try not feeling dopey, or worried you'll sound like a faux-Native, hippie freak. Try thinking, *My mother is someone I love and rely on. Who angers me. Who I don't understand. Am tied to by fate. Who's complex. Ferocious. Whom I fear. Am in awe of.*

Try: *My brother is a bird of prey. My brother's a bracing, cold river.* Then what?

Go further.

Try River seen from a plane as *Blood-moving-in-veins.*

A river bent in an S as *Snake.* Not snaking. But *Snake.* If intensely bright—way brighter than a black racer in sun—say *A snake in flames, a burning snake.* The language here is not fanciful but real as a twisted river burning, the Cuyahoga (Iroquois, *crooked river*), sludge-filled, oily, and ruined. By the late '60s, nothing lived in that open sewer. Not a sunfish. Not a black snake. And finally, one fire, the thirteenth recorded since the 1850s, was enough. (You can trace the origins of the Environmental Protection Agency to this time and, in part, to this place.) The Cuyahoga's not yet recovered, but so far, sixty species of fish have been counted and in healthy sections, beavers, herons, and eagles have been spotted nesting along the banks.

Kids fishing or paddling along today don't know the moon once effloresced, and sun rainbowed up in oily swells. That the air was sulfur. That once we made of a gift, a sewer.

It's hard to see *Bright skin of water prickling in wind* as *Cicatrice*.

MYTHOLOGICAL FIGURES IN THE BACKGROUND

Once I stayed at a house where the owners kept a stone bird in a cage. The bird's absolute stillness, the impossibility of song felt cautionary. Wherever I sat, I couldn't get away from it, I mean the old and very real truth—that people get turned from themselves into many things—salt, nightingales, gold, the loveliest of lakeside flowers. And their names become a way to think about seasons, the sky, failure, luck, circumstance.

Look anywhere, at anything, and you'll find yourself there; the world offers us to ourselves at every turn: *Midas touch*. *Narcissist*. Metaphors are terribly generous that way.

ADVENTURES IN BEAUTY

Once, a friend, reacting to a tickle on her arm, saw she had smacked a lacewing—green-filigreed and sheer as a breath. "Oh, you're so beautiful, I'm sorry," she said, before finishing it off.

As if its beauty might have saved it.

What then of stinkbugs and worms, silverfish, earwigs (awful, shivery name), the armored and pincered, jiggly and larval, slick with ooze, sweating in sun—the uglies removed without hesitation. Or opossums, those quiet, shy creatures as smart as dogs, who can't overcome their pointy, ghost faces and needly teeth, whose bright black eyes are *cold* and *beady*—the same dark eyes that in dolphins signal the presence of soul.

A beautiful thing makes a live air, looking upon it fills the eye up, and as the eye rests on the graceful or lush, the heart swells, the breath slows, and in beholding, one's strength is confirmed. A beautiful thing flatters us into care.

A slug also catches the eye, reflecting sunlight like a prismy tear—which we meet with no desire at all, no urge to scoop up and tuck under a shady leaf, to "make a dwelling in the evening air, / in which being there together is enough." Slugs, too, keep us back, but skinless, unshelled, like stuff meant to be washed from the body, their softness is a contamination, an outward sign of an inward fragility (unnervingly tender, like liver or brains on display in the butcher's case). In motion, a slug is peristaltic, embarrassing. It can't rush away. It has nowhere to hide.

Or let me try this: it's not the beautiful's need to be cared for, but its independence that beckons and holds us. The beautiful possesses an abundance of form-color-scent-gesture, and with such riches is sufficient unto itself. Looking on, gathering the radiance in, it's we who are fed on its plenty. And thus inessential, extraneous to it, like any discounted lover, we're moved—compelled even—to sidle up and be near.

Or because "beauty is the beginning of a terror we are just able to bear," the sidling up must be done with care. Beauty as proto, early-stage, fresh. Not yet an excess, not yet the sublime—those full-force gales, deep gorges, and dark, brooding, overhung moods.

If one is moved to incline towards beauty, willing even to be wounded by it—that brief "Oh" in "Oh, you're so beautiful"— then the quick recoil at the sight of a slug is a kind of protection. A slug is already on the decline, a slippery clot, a leak threatening borders. It melts and sags. Confronted with the delicacy of a slug—how under the slightest nudge it'll wince—something deep in the body takes over and we veer away. Or, if intent on hastening the end, we dissolve them with handfuls of salt.

A beautiful, say, zinnia in bloom is alert and upright. There's spine in its comport, no hunching, no crawling along on its belly. Propped in a vase, a cut flower asserts the absolute present, intensifies it, makes of itself an extravagance.

Easy to say a day's beautiful—sun, nothing cruel in the wind, a sky that shouts its color out, fingerings of breeze, exhilarants of scent. All the component parts are upfront, and lit. A gray sky has its brightness, though it doesn't impose. It's not so full of glare and assertion. Gray is the register of underseen things, of tinctures and compounds. It's not on the scale of beautiful/ugly, it occupies instead a dimension, like epochs at the heart of a stone.

"Beauty is truth, truth beauty," being "all / Ye know on earth, and all ye need to know" is a comfort. An assertion sliding between fixed points. Gray, though, makes you look harder—what *else* is there?—squint until you skid off the track, where those creatures who live neither-here-nor-there hide—edge of a cliff, side of the highway, in gaps and passes. Transitional spots are neither safe nor contained.

And there, in the regions where things unsettle, you might linger until the lace on a wing turns back to veins, till what looked like a simple head clarifies and you see in its place a welter of eyes. Angled just so in soft, plain light—a light that does not desiccate—a slug might iridesce, its eyes incline toward your words and breath, its gaze be gently inquisitive. There would be no start or end to your sight. The jesses would slip from slug and lacewing, and in falling away their forms be released, the language of measurement break into pieces, and each moment of seeing be again its own shining grunt of creation.

BRIEF TREATISE AGAINST IRONY

The opposite of irony is nakedness. To be available to the eyes of others. So instead of ironic furnishings—coconut-shell lampshades for the tourist you're not, each Aloha, Willkommen thing worse than the next, that's the point—a person buys a painting she can afford and hangs it in her house. Gives it something called *pride of place*. In this, the very rich resemble the not-so-rich-at-all: taste displayed according to means. What you see is what they like. Ugly, vapid, tender, exquisite: you're free to judge. Such things in a frame, on a shelf front and center, crass/gilded, frank/quiet, are defenseless, sent forth without armor, or veils.

*

Sincerity can't be applied like a salve, or plaster, or be arranged to countervail irony. That won't cure it. Sincerity doesn't take measures to appear to be, or to seem. Asked to prove itself, its voice squeaks. Its eyes water, walking into the wind. In rough surf, it erodes. In heat, it sweat-stains. Its gauges work. It's accurate. To be an apple tree in fall, to fully enter the realm of gold, to be right up against the no-longer-green—that move can't be scripted. Sincerity isn't in service of. A tree doesn't will itself to turn, to feel darkness and chill crenellate its leaves, then let go. Trees give over. That phrase *the promise of spring*? Trees really believe it.

*

Irony masks. It prepares for, in advance. No one sees its heart adjusting, dimming, tamping. Irony won't admit to *heart* (too messy, percussive). It ducks into corners and drops from eaves. It sniffs for changes in weather so as to be first to deflect. Irony's a stick figure in an oversized coat. It refuses the pleasures of shivering, the anticipation of a warm house after taking the garbage out—in a T-shirt, in an ice storm—those small restorations, minor hardships that stoke gratitude.

*

Irony rules its subjects like a monarch—the fiefdom-centric variety, not the butterfly hereing and thereing, looping up, ferrying a clutch of sweetness, alighting on ripening buds with gifts, such delicate work, the scattering of gold.

*

Irony's internal compass is wobbly. It suffers from tracking a northernish star. Irony references, cites, points to—and in doing so, advances not at all. Each year its finger grows longer and thinner, as pale and slippery as a stalactite. Its weather is clammy. Its system low-pressure. It suffers not the exertions of sun, which shines equally on the deserving and the not-so, the vast sea of us all. Irony isn't equipped to navigate rough democracies.

Irony has no hidden reserves. It sits and stews. If "boredom is an opportunity; a state in which hope is being secretly negotiated" (tacked on my bulletin board, author unknown)—then irony's not fit to negotiate. (But wait, I looked it up just now . . . it's from a review of philosopher/psychologist Adam Phillips! Irony would do well to get excited about discoveries, be agog, still, at the powers of the web.) Irony would do well to search for . . . *something*. And let disappointment come if it will. Maybe envy. Squirm in frustration. Because none of this—boredom, disappointment—will kill you. Out of real need, or absence, or tedium, irony might *make* something.

*

Irony is the outward sign of a feeling one's trying not to have. The adult version of yanking your crush's braid on the playground. *See*, it announces, *I'm not interested!* The wide-lapel suit, worn not-seriously. The studiously untended mutton chops.

The song "How Deep Is Your Love," though I hated it, was part of the soundtrack of my thirteenth year, and my long stay in the hospital. I loved a boy then, who was having the same back surgery. He was funny and gentle; I missed him when one of us was wheeled away for a procedure. His family lived nearby in the South Bronx and they always brought lots of food and shared with my parents. I know we kissed. How did we manage that, both of us stuck in body casts?

After, we wrote a few letters, but we never saw each other again.

I can't imagine that song played, say, at a dinner party, the table set with wineglasses from *Bea's & Roger's* (that double possessive!) *Aniversery Cruise* (and that *spelling*), *1977*.

I don't imagine anyone liked the smell of coal trains, blackening the Russian stations of their childhood. But much is returned by way of it, admixed with sausages, perfume, cigarettes. The most unlikely song or whiff will guard a past and sail it back when you're least expecting it. Thus a person might find herself in tears, right there in the dentist's chair, the classic rock station playing endless Bee Gees. Or when passing a newly tarred street in Ohio, a whole country, an era, Moskovsky Station in winter, steams up in the summer heat.

*

Irony has no sense of time. So what might have been meaningful once—blue Snoopy lunch box, his gladness at the midday reunion—is wiped away by irony's taking it up again as a find, an amusing accessory. Irony opposes the heirloom, the keepsake. It turns away from good leftovers. Won't cook up a fresh, fancy thing on a special occasion. A thing that might fail, burn, collapse. Require the guests' good cheer and willingness to order last-minute pizza, be part of a wholly disastrous dinner but a great story ever after—i.e., *history*.

*

Irony travels in one direction, around and around an inner circle. A kids' TV show I used to watch, *Zoom*, ran a skit with a character called Fannee Doolee. She liked any person, place, thing, or concept with double letters in it, but hated its non-double-lettered equivalent, so "Fannee Doolee likes sweets but hates candy." You could figure out how to play the game if you watched and listened for a while, but it wasn't apparent right away. Tuning in every week, you had to suss out the hints. Something was there to be decoded. It was a *challenge*. A *riddle*. (Once you figured it out, you could send in your own example to be read on TV.) A riddle is an invitation, a game about roaming in language, while irony cordons off play. Admits only the knowing few. The tickets are invisible. You can't buy them anywhere. In this way, irony both suggests and thwarts travel.

Its inside track is a very small circle.

*

There is nothing animal about irony. Animal *is*. Last week, when I was walking my dog in the woods (urban woods with nearby streets), we were set upon by a pack; at first, dog by dog, they were tame, sniffing and romping and chasing Ruby. Then something turned. A mind like a wind blew though the dogs, gathered strength like a wave from far off, and rose up. It was as slow and elemental as a tide. Once it entered, the conversion was swift. They closed in on my dog, growling and jumping and wouldn't listen to their owner's shrill whistle. We slipped through a hole in the fence just in time.

The dogs weren't kidding. And they weren't angry. Just

subject to a force that turned them deeply back into themselves. It was an amazing thing to watch: instinct finding a vein and entering. In them was nothing cruel or trained. They made an old shape, an organism that worked as one, which was beautiful and terrifying to see.

*

Irony lets you know it *knows*.

Look, I'm from New York. That "We've seen it all" attitude? There's something to it, beyond arrogance. If you've seen it all—in the course of a recent hour, two Great Danes in mink coats (*full length*, I guess you'd say), a guy selling dentures from a backpack ("unused")—then irony's passé. Something else overtakes—older than irony. Brisker. Sharper. The daily surreal. The absurd. All the infinite, unpredictable ways to be human. It's New York: you do what you want. Ride your bike in a bikini with a snake as a necklace (it was hot that day, she was en route to the pet sitter, and *he really likes to go for rides*.) The closer you come to the absurd, the more irony looks kind of homegrown, provincial. All that time put in to make an impression, all that care taken to seem not to care.

There's a moment in Nabokov's memoir, *Speak, Memory*, where he gets actually angry with those who can't detect his special variety of immigrant loss: "The following passage is not for the general reader, but for the particular idiot who, because he lost a fortune in some crash, thinks he understands me. My old (since 1917) quarrel with the Soviet dictatorship is wholly unrelated to any question of property. My contempt for the émigré who 'hates the Reds' because they 'stole' his money and land is complete. The nostalgia I have been cherishing all these years is a hypertrophied sense of lost childhood, not sorrow for lost banknotes." Irony doesn't immigrate. All that *contempt*, *nostalgia*, real *sorrow*—not safe passage.

Of course, irony's all over New York, in so many forms and registers: those giant, balloonish, steel bunny sculptures; or a boutique's curated collection of vintage Mr. Bubble, Pop-Tart, *Jetsons* T-shirts. Both sort of, kind of make you laugh, but not too much. Maybe once. Not out loud. More a mumbly appraisal-sound.

The absurd's both public and shared. Like water fountains. Like air.

The absurd understands brevity, longing, how much is thwarted or unmet, or met only partly. It acknowledges the infinite scheme, confirms the stark/tender, sad/sweet endless ways to be human—*counter, original, spare, strange*, as Hopkins wrote—and the lightness attending that recognition; the flash of all that is perishable. The absurd allows for quick glance exchanged with seatmate on bus, appreciation, *something*, for the old guy whose leashed monkey totes his own little backpack. That brief moment, I don't know what it is, except abundant in New York, and available in so many versions, tongues, flavors: Puerto Rican. Senegalese. Korean. Etc. The quick-unaccountable. The fragile-but-ancient.

Ironic is no one's country of origin. Oh, I *get* it alright. It's just not interesting. It won't be amazed. It won't admit fear. There isn't a bit of longing in it. No danger. No failure. No dream.

WALK WITH
SNOWY THINGS

That wasn't snow.

But it should've been, looks to be, lacy with dirt, side of the road, gouged and firmed by the melt/freeze cycle. What was it I passed, sixty-something degrees in late December—not proper snow but a snarl of gray cotton, scoured and cinched, in the snowy habit of catching flung dirt.

And what's this, a block later, a snow-colored eggshell (also wrong in December), resting as fallen shells rest in the grass, gently and up—though what happens with eggs is not at all gentle, that breaking apart of a known world for another. The not-eggshell is a packing chip, so like the half shell I loved as a kid, all that delicious foam for licking, Venus's floating hair for braiding and I'd help her down into scallopy waves and swim with her, body to body, fully the animal I knew myself to be.

There's more not-snow on the east side of the neighborhood—this handful (why so much cotton today?) spotted with blood like a sick x-rayed lung, part of a rough tableau on the grass, sifted round with packets of sugar, a burned plastic bottle and inside it, a needle (addicts, too, have their weird, tidy gestures like anyone fitting the cap on a jar before tossing it out). Hard to imagine this wasn't arranged—just come upon, the story so clear. Light on the shoelace tourniquet, sugar for cutting, matches for cooking. Someone's next moment gauzed up in this spot, a sweet blameless hour, soft, with no edges hastening back, the fog-world easeful and grainy and fat—and here's the full mess of that peace.

Around the corner, a single not-snowflake in a sidewalk crack where it won't unmelt, whatever it is, confetti far from its parade, or a fallen snow-planet. It's not *meaning* I'm looking for in the way these things come, if indeed they come from anywhere, or are bent on arriving and being seen. All I know is, I'm the site-of. I'm where they meet. Under pretense of snow. Suggestion of snow. Under snow's wing or a snow-scene setting up, calling its characters in, down, and *here*. Practice snow. Snow attempts and alerts. Where the white bits found and arranged their thinking, patterned themselves into an order, I get to be a gathering spot, like a ring of rocks in clear, shallow water where trout float over their pearly young.

Such are the happier snow-like things. Snow-like betters. Stuff not made of waste or grief. This dandelion held in its final white phase, unblown, geodesic, still wrong in December, but so unto itself there's no need to translate it out of garbage and junk. Either way, though, so much is given. All these versions of looking into what's always been there and suddenly, the filling commences. There are relations, one comes as another, things are rekinned.

A vision is nothing a person chooses—a vision comes flying,

comes landing, unwalled, light laved if you make of yourself a hospitable place that won't melt a thing, step on, step over, or proceed with the business of a day, which so often means: nothing to see here, keep going, enough with the stopping and sniffing, move on.

But if things pile up, as they do if allowed, then, here we go:

Tufts of white dog-hair combed out or shed. Husky fur. Collie fur. Dry and nest-ready. Once I found a nest made entirely of human hair. So perfectly bark-colored, soft and expandable, that air-and-light weave, imagine how easy to work with, a dream!— though as a nest, a total mistake: too sheer, no sticks or mud mingled in. There it was, the extravagant thought, or evidence of a mind being new to a task, technique coming clear after going so wrong, the bird-light blinking on, the way obvious now—a bird reviewing its failed, fallen nest, head bent to the side (you've done this, too, revising a thought)—something like *Oh. Right. I get it . . . twigs. Then work some hair in—but only a little.*

Here's a piece of popcorn ducking behind a blade of grass. It looks at first like chewed gum or a molar and then more like cotton, but raw, from the field. The first time I saw the real thing, outside Tuscaloosa, I asked my friend to stop the truck, right there, side of the road, so I could get out and touch it. I was in my midforties. A mid-forty-year-old person who'd never seen cotton—not those gray photos in the *Britannica* list of major state crops, not packed tight in a blue first aid box, but a form that moved into the neck and back, bent a body to the hard task, ached in the gut—and then it became a whole different drive, my fresh cotton rough in its boll in my hand, the weight of it gone entirely strange, very dense, sort of cold. Like holding a bullet for the first time.

This is bird shit, rain-thinned on the sidewalk, a splotchy snow-shadow, gathering, as all this stuff is, for the eye training toward it. Offerings that come once the frame is constructed. Likenesses finding a home. Vision forming. Out in a field where I'm to meet it. Out in a field where I'm also the field. I don't know what the moment's thinking, but it's telling itself. Things are alive. Without me, and within. There is nothing shut up or remote, but everywhere is "cloth'd with what itself adorns." I mean I'm getting rearranged by all the seeing and being seen.

Turning the corner, this little stone rabbit—corralled with stone frogs in a garden scene—is hunched in a position called sniff-the-ground-and-show-off-my-white-tail-forever. The white tail is more cotton and up comes the moment when, as a kid, the words first pulled apart—*cotton* and *tail*, and it wasn't one single blur-of-a-word, *cottontail*, just some sounds that meant *rabbit*. How often I missed things so clear to everyone else. Adult versions persist: still having a hard time pronouncing *waistcoat* as *weskit*, and remembering to drop the *c* in *victuals* so as to align with those who know *vittles*, *say vittles*, and mean it. Or, as we said growing up, "the roast pan"—since it belonged to the roast alone, and was hauled out only a few times a year. A friend corrected me—supposed to be "roasting pan," but I'm sticking with the original, my language: roast pan—talisman bringing my grandmother back every December, her kitchen, the heat, the big dinner coming.

So goes my white-spotted world, neighborhood at least, all the found things that come to me. Come to be held. Hear that? *Beheld?*—the intensified form, the stand-back-so-as-to-see-the-light version, or angle that promises by holding a thing, I'll be held by it, that attention swings both ways at once. And what to *do* with that thought?

I think "go on for a bit" is a reasonable plan. I'm nearly home now.

Here's a pod from a black locust tree whose inner white bed isn't full white but cut-with-cream, fuzzed like young antlers in sun, the whole thing softening me so unexpectedly that I can't tell which came first, the pod's velvety sheen, or that it approached without words and went something like—*Here's how you feel about that beloved friend you hardly ever get to see.* And in this next pod, one loaded with seeds—*here's* how you feel with her around: multiplied and fed, loaved and fished! Then comes a compact pod-for-two, which might also be a dinner table, a diner table is more precise, since we like to eat bacon and eggs together. Or, it's a skiff—*skiff* is old-timey, or *bark*, or *dory*, or best of all *coracle*—since these fit exactly her sensibility and she'd get a kick out of it if I said, pointing down with my toe, *Look, there's our boat, come on, get in!* Because you can do that with some people, row so easily far from shore.

So here, this pod is how distance breaks up, loss softens, leads back, little gift embedded in litter, in leaves—it's how a letter the day wrote me arrived. All these letters arriving. I keep being read to. So much comes in and arranges (today, whitely), comes shining, comes brimmed, in pangs and shocks. Alongside-running, on rounded, fat, wet—or steep, spired moments. So much figures forth. I must be wanting. I believe it takes a very great yearning to call down so great a giving.

BLOODSPOTS (1)

I followed the spots, dime-sized and evenly spaced for ten sidewalk squares, and then came to a splash where the blood looked poured out from a height. After that, the spots stopped. Everything stopped.

And everything turned.

My assumption came clear—that the origin of the blood was back where I began, and I was following it *to* somewhere. How sure I'd been of my own cartographics, my cosmologics, my own little Earth on its own contained course, until the end roared up as beginning instead.

All inversions are reckonings.

A sign was posted there at the end-which-was-really-the-beginning: "Being happy is the most beautiful thing!" How you read it depends on inflection, where the voice comes to rest, where you make the voice land.

So: at the tail of the sentence (on "beautiful thing") the exclamation weighing in would be a cruelty to someone grieving.

Or land on the beginning (on "happy"—being *happy* is the most beautiful thing) and it's a kind of sloganeering, meaning "replace the importance of being beautiful with the act of being happy instead."

Or hover mid-line and accent "the most" ("the" pronounced "thee") so that, as a measure among other beautiful things, *happy* is the final word on the matter.

The eye rests, the voice lands—and meanings turn. You get to turn them.

Say: *It's a windy day*. Or: "*When I stand upright in the wind / My bones turn to dark emeralds.*"

One's a fact and sure of itself.

The other describes being found and rearranged.

BLOODSPOTS (II)

Coming slant in sheets, steaming the sidewalk midsummer, then stopping—the first rain since the murder on University Parkway. Across the street from my son's girlfriend's house. A few miles from ours. Two blocks from another friend, whose blood I've seen, body I've tended—that complicated wound on her hip the antibiotics couldn't fix. Years ago now. She stayed for a while in an oxygen chamber, maybe it helped, she can't remember. When she came home that first week, I'd go to her, and as dinner heated and the girls ran around, I took off the bandage. Cleaned at the edges. Replaced the dressing. It was so deep the bone flashed like a moon between night hills.

Here on the sidewalk, rain kindled up all these live reds—root of an oak scuffed clean of its bark, big hearted coleus, gas-and-electric flag marking a line, plastic bag stuck to the curb and translucing. Then a few rusty spots shone up through a puddle. No, the *feel* of finding them lit, no real shining went on. They embellished nothing. They marked an event but could not say the story. A guy came towards me with his collie. He knew what I was looking for. Because he was, too. As we passed each other, there it was, all the mutual knowing, and we looked away fast, no words for the passing, the rain gone, the blood dimming, and we were ashamed of living like that—as if days go on, which they do, and for being the ones who, by living, confirm it.

BLOODSPOTS (III)

"Hello, this is an important message from the Baltimore City Police Department. Last night, on May 22, 2017, at approximately 3:10 a.m. there was a homicide committed in the 5100 block of York Road. We're asking anyone who has information or knows someone who has information to call Detective . . . (etc., etc.). . . . Thank you for your help."

Some neighborhood homicides generate a robocall and others don't. I have no idea why.

And on the day after, where was I? I got up early and worked till noon. Went to the drugstore (5200 block) and had lunch with my son. We talked of our neighborhood's various boundaries, and yes, we covered the pertinent topics—redlining, blockbusting, turf wars, and so on and so forth with the institutions of higher injustice. Of the city's hundreds of microcommunities, ours is described as "friendly, affordable, diverse." A block away, York Road remains one of the sharpest East/West divides (East communities get no adjectives on the real estate sites). And the blood would be *where*, I wondered, on which side? And the location, evidence of what?

I know myself well enough to say that the searching itself is a particular method: I look to figure out why I'm looking.

Let me triangulate my position. Coming up to the corner under review, York and Winston, there's the community garden (Westsiders' project). Across the street (E) is Value Village, where most recently I got my son a pair of good winter boots and a watch for myself. Everyone (E & W) shops there. If you turn back from Value Village, pass the garden (tangle of weekend weeding awaits) and head west a block, there's our house. Backyard planted up with offerings from friends, so when I look out I see their faces in hostas, hydrangeas, and black-eyed Susans. My dog's running around now with her new pal next door. Who else have I seen here? Owls, foxes, opossums, hawks. Go further (W) down the street and it's even greener—a small patch of real woods, home or rest stop for the abovementioned. A little creek banking along till it hits a drainpipe and emerges again en route to the falls. Black buzzards on the college library's roof. Buttercup Forest so named by (W) kids, the ground entirely yellow in spring. Patch of hillside let go to Peace Meadow, complete with new plaque ("Lord make me an instrument of Thy peace," etc.) I stop by and read often. Sledding hill. Frisbee/soccer/dog run field. Closer to York, group homes of many sorts. Popeyes. McDonald's. Medical clinic.

Such is the micro Western front.

To the East, an abundance of liquor stores, braiding salons, corner takeouts, methadone clinic.

I don't know what the blood will say. Or if I find it, what I'll do. Out here now, on the corner of York and Winston (W), the sounds I gather extend my looking: a nearby cardinal's *please-please-please-please birdie-birdie-birdie* (I can see his throat pulsing in a McDonald's tree). Bass-line barking the dogs lay in. Something off-loaded, dropped very hard and over and over, which could be gunshot, but isn't. This echo's entirely different. To describe a fleet-bodied, there-and-gone light, Emily Dickinson wrote, "Noons report away"—and so must've known her gun sounds, too. A word used well is many-realmed and maps in all directions at once. So, *report* unfurls further—as in noons *tell about themselves*, or *show up for duty*.

I did not hear last night's shots, but on other nights they're very clear.

Still, I think of them as *out there*.

Here on the corner, a bike with two LOVE emblazoned saddlebags goes by. A couple with matching T-shirts (Thing 1 and Thing 2) walks into the (W) clinic. A leafy branch the length of me in the middle of the street, run over and flattened, goes on shining with all the wet pressed out of it.

Some yellow crime scene tape still attached to the lamppost is blowing like a kite tail in wind (E)—so I'm close. It's a busy place, York and Winston:

Corner salon selling Virgin Hair (E) and on the window above the salon, the words TAX_ O_ _ ICE stenciled in black (once I sat in my car for a good ten minutes filling in the unlettered bits).

The remodeled Westside McDonald's (where once I Heimliched an Eastside baby choking on a piece of hamburger).

Gas station (E) with its double-take sign: *Quality Is Not an Option, Expect It*. The tattered rock roses in front—gas station owner's attempt to spiff up and appease (the Westside) neighbors upset about dealing on premises, trash collection, the murder there almost exactly a year ago.

Here on the corner, as I'm trained up to do, I'm sifting the simultaneities: (E) teenagers on motorbikes screaming down York, a version of skateboarders at the pricey Westside Jesuit college—where on one of the buildings is carved a line of Gerard Manley Hopkins's: "The world is charged with the grandeur of God." When I'm waiting for the light to change, I say it aloud and run through the refractions: *charged*, as with responsibility, to care for; *charged*, as in electrified, lit; *charged*, meaning *run at* or *run through*, the known world taken by surprise and pierced; *charged* as if for a crime committed and the world made to pay for it, some kind of guilt-feel, which I can't make sense of, but still hovers.

I call this all *my neighborhood* when I'm talking to anyone not from here, unfamiliar with the precision-carved nature of things. *Where I buy my clothes* (E) and *grow my food* (W) makes it sound like a village, self-reliant, contained, with a town hall near and market stalls and everyone knows each other's kin. And that last part's true, but East keeps to East kin and West to West. I'm looking around on the East side of the street now, where I don't have much reason to be, where the rules are nowhere inscribed but govern—at the moment, quietly, except for gas getting and Value Village shopping, *This isn't where you belong,* they say. And here's a more profound version of the invisibles and unspokens: The other day I stopped to talk with my neighbor a few houses down, who had a load of yard brush to get rid of. He told me it would cost sixty-eight dollars to bring to the city dump with his little trailer, and I said why not just stuff it in the college dumpster around the corner, that's what I (white) do. As in, *Oh wow, sorry officer, ran out of lawn bags, didn't realize, won't do it again.* That's how I'd proceed. *Hmm*, he said, quiet and looking off, the feel of his calculation clear: in this, his own neighborhood, that's not how it would go for him.

This isn't easy territory to read. The elements keep sliding around: how that *auk-auk-auk* bird call might also be (as day is done, and dark comes on) blood clotting up in a throat from a chest wound.

Nothing is still or unto itself. Meanings regroup and retrofit, layer up and multiply. To read the land like a poem (not make it *poetic*—what we say when things go ethery) is to read for the all-dimensions-at-once sensation. To listen in archeologically. To navigate constellationally. So a singular moment overrides its fixed place.

Three years ago, when the city exploded, just after Freddie Gray died, I met up with some (W) neighbors who intended to help clean up the shattered storefronts on York, a few blocks from here. We went as a group, some with peace signs, all with brooms, trash bags, and shovels—and as we crossed Woodbourne Avenue, a guy whose business was interrupted looked up and spit and said, "Yeah, fuck your peace."

The offence of peace. Imported. Marched in. So earnest in its imposition.

Fuck your peace: like any poem, unfurling the vast energies within.

Here on the corner (W) three red lines look like the blood I'm looking for, but I translate them back: surveyors' marks for new drainpipes. Then a few steps over in front of McDonald's, near bus stop and trash can, fresh scrub marks on the sidewalk, dark at the edges like a sunset cloud. A gray dove of the Eurasian variety, not the white kind with olive branch, lands in the center and pecks at a roll. A small tangle of hair is blowing in circles (in Baltimorese, a *tumbleweave*), taking up with newspaper, half a blunt, soda can. Everything mingling, touching, reordering.

So, here they are, the bloodspots I sought—here and not East. Nothing's *encroaching*. They're not a West anomaly. If where I live is to compass more than one street, I have to say *at my doorstep* not-figuratively. Any last-ditch efforts at elsewhereing—*it was 3 a.m. and I'm never out then* or *he knew the assailant* or *deal gone bad*—aren't working. None of it's working. Elsewhereing unpoems a place. And illiterates me.

BLOODSPOTS (IV): CODA

The late August heat stoppers in tight after rain, no relief, but everything shines, everything smells of fresh mud and worms. About ten steps ahead of me, a low-circling hawk dives into tall grass, lifts off with a mouse, and flies it up to a crook in a nearby white pine. It's so quiet I can hear the bones snap, the beak click. I watch the red shoulders tense and release (hawk patience and neatness), the dipping in and picking so deft. Barest breeze ruffling underwing. Breast curve white against the rough bark. When the bodies shift, wet needles let down their rain.

On my way back, the hawk's already flown. In the empty space, sun falls on the spot where I know the blood is. Someone climbing this tree on a bright day in fall wouldn't notice a thing, the red long gone to shadow or moss. Persistent damp. Mottled bark. But there it was, the ease, the dive so precise (no grazing or clipping), the lifting-as-one (not a thing murked, no slang for the killing), the piercing and tearing was urgent and bloody, and—no proper animal would think to note this—there was no anger, waste, or meanness.

ON SHADOWS:
SOME INVESTIGATIONS

What's in a shadow? Not the stories colors tell (how hair can honey or silver in sunlight, what that red rock the size of a buffalo heart said). A shadow, in fear, can't deepen its pink like a flounder or squid. It won't go opaque like a chip of beach glass or behave like a plum clouding with bloom. A shadow can't bronze a leaf in fall (though neither one holds on very long). No iridescing like oyster shells, the wings of cicadas, gasoline puddles.

Shadows begin by leaning into the west, cinch up at noon, and by dusk reconstitute, holding their breath until disappearing low and thin in the east. All day long shadows rehearse their leaving.

How to move through the world with yours? Gently. Shadows are porous and, though hinged to the body, are easily overcome by the darkness of others. In the postures of shadows are expressions distilled—reticence before crossing a threshold; some hunching or bristling; your dark, upright joy thrown onto the street. Such intimacy with muddy curb, fire hydrant, pile of trash! A shadow rests on anything. So deftly fills the space it's poured into, alights on dry land or water or rock, and leaves no print at all.

Passes over and leaves not a trace.

Shadows are tests of specialized seeing: at what micromoment does a subject's bearing turn from *bent to a task* to *grieving*? From *hide-and-seek counting* to *on the knees, praying*. Shadows won't return a frank gaze; you have to suss out their inclinations— look up from your book and see in the tilt of your beloved's head (projected there, against the wall), degrees of mood, that something has changed. Voices override and insist, but the body's inflection won't lie.

Reconsider the usual attitudes toward shadows: dark-therefore-evil, while light's the pure good. How sharp distinctions are called *night-and-day*. It's hard to shift conventional stances what with language like *shadowy* and *shadowed by*. Followed fast by *the light of reason*. Shadows are really hybrid things, so those foxes/birds/rabbits crossing tent flaps and night walls? All born of a flashlight's beam and your hand.

A shadow's a form of relief. The eye can sink into it, relax and unfocus—no pixels apparent, no zillions of tiny particles zinging. A kitchen table is wild with emptiness, but we, untrained for conceptual shimmer, agree to see only heft and stillness and call our tables *reliable objects*.

But a shadow *is* reliable and steady. Its edges don't bleed. It won't crest its banks. It's a tidy leak. Shadows suggest certain lines or states are terribly fragile, mysteriously easeful—say, the one between Sleep and Death.

Intending to stay in motion (light at their backs, conditions just right), shadows end up, despite their restlessness, *gone*— gathered back to their source, in the way all passionate makers of atmosphere use themselves up entirely.

LOSS COLLECTION

SPARROW

Who cleared the bird from the stony path, bird I was watching become something else, its wet feathers matting then drying and parting back to skin? In a few more months, the ribs would've been a house framed out, barrel staves, then once the spine showed, the keel of a skiff. Already wind was passing through the very body it used to lift.

Such strange reversals the end brings.

The bird was one of my private measures of time bent to its work, paring, reducing, and recomposing—those colonies below digging in and fattening on the body. I was tracking increments, how the bird wore its days. Or days wore a bird. I kept it as evidence of one of the ways the world goes on without me. That the world goes on without me is an old and familiar shiver. Lying in bed on a summer night and hearing the older kids still at their games, would join with a flash of kids in Japan on the far side of the globe, rising and eating their morning soup. I was not moved to slip out to play then, or pinch an arm and confirm myself. I wanted only to be-and-not-be simultaneously, for as long as the displacement lasted.

With the bird gone now, what's missing is a way to reset the day. I keep checking the path for the cycle ongoing: a being turned toward becoming again. Recently, in that spot, one rock balanced just so on another became a dark breast, feathered with dampness. A tab from a coffee cup was a beak. There was some solace in imagining, but without the body, time's renegade—it can't be illustrated by a diminishing wing. Its increments are not en route to anything.

OPEN SPACE

Spots that look bare at first—stretch of back, upper arm—are, if you slow your looking way down, sites of endless microscenes: angles thrown by sudden flexing, shadows cast by turning and bending, folds lit by sweat, outcrops catching wind. Once, the eye could rest on these. Sip from. Take in. Those spots on the body so full of suggestion, that inclined toward or beckoned seem now occupied with Tweety Birds, anchors, names of beloveds. All those images staking claims. A rise of muscle, like a hill once learned by climbing and roaming, is real estate. A place settled and named, with monuments, plaques, and private museums. It's always been the habit of conquering imaginations to call a place *empty*, and build there.

For a taste of what used to be, you can visit tallgrass prairie preserves in Kansas and Oklahoma, spaces much like the unmarked body—efforts of conservation, and rare.

FIRE

Of one form of lost intimacy, Thoreau wrote: "I sometimes left a good fire when I went to take a walk in a winter afternoon; and when I returned, three or four hours afterward, it would still be alive and glowing. My house was not empty though I was gone. . . . It was I and Fire that lived there." Then things changed at Walden Pond. "The next winter I used a small cooking-stove . . . but it did not keep fire as well as the open fireplace. Cooking was then, for the most part, no longer a poetic, but merely a chemic process. It will soon be forgotten, in these days of stoves, that we used to roast potatoes in the ashes, after the Indian fashion. The stove not only took up room . . . but it concealed the fire, and I felt as if I had lost a companion."

Such are small reveries improved away.

And what of other losses sustained? At the moment plumbing moved inside, I imagine I'd have felt keenly the absence of wells—the thrice daily (*thrice* itself gone!) chore of fetching, the load awkward and heavy, but on the way there and back, a quiet all to myself; the scrape of the empty bucket descending; the plunge-and-fill sounds; the crank tense and rope spooling; my face in ripples surfacing; the overfull splashing on legs in summer, so sweet.

What's the word for an elegy that mourns a thing it never knew?

My tallow candle, its buttery crackle.

My jeweled preserves on a pantry shelf in winter light.

TREES

Once that sound, wind-through-trees, was *a forest breathing*. A body moving through woods understood it. Breathing meant many things: signs of rain or evening coming, early notice of seasons turning, a density of pines giving way to meadow. But now, even if you stand very still—in deep winter, high summer, it hardly matters—what you're hearing is likely distant traffic, planes above clouds, or generators. Not a deep sigh. Not a thought humming. To think that a forest might breathe now is a *fancy*—a state "modified by that empirical phenomenon of the will," as Coleridge said. Whereas it used to take *imagination*, that "higher form," the "living power and prime agent of all human perception." So went the Romantic notion that, by overcoming intellection and knowing the world to be animate, we might regain for brief spots of time all that's been worn so thoroughly away.

The force that renders land, water, and trees *quaint* ("charming in an old-fashioned way") settles in. Settling controls and legislates. To suspect that a thought might be called *quaint* cinches in imagining. Dams the changeable truths of a stream. Shrivels a phrase like *the wings of trees*. *Quaint* won't let a body see green-in-flight, or suggest the song of budding pears is in any way pinkly audible.

DODO

Once men with their dogs, cats, rats, and pigs overtook the quiet island of Mauritius, the Dodo disappeared. In one 1622 account, a whole flock of Dodos, hearing the squawking of a single bird, rushed to the scene and all were captured, snatched easily by hungry Dutch sailors. With no natural predators, safe and content on their wooded island, Dodos nested on the ground and spent their days eating and sleeping. Though capable of running, there was no need. And their beaks, though hooked and powerful, found no occasion for self-defense. Imagine a flightless, three-foot-tall bird, heavy and round, with a tufty tail and afterthought wings coming easily up to you, tipping its curious, bald head to one side, fixing you in its bright yellow eye. Imagine it eating from your hand, or working beside you plucking crabs at low tide. Or that by watching and tagging along, you'd be led to all the fruit you'd need.

Speculation about the Dodo's name confirms a very different stance: perhaps derived from the Portuguese *doudo* or *doido* meaning "fool" or "crazy." Or from the Dutch *dodoor* (sluggard) or *dodaars* (fat ass). As late as 1766, Linnaeus coined *Didus ineptus*—"Inept Dodo." And still, today, *Dodo* means "addled, laughable, dumb."

And what might be the Linnaean for *one who blames a thing for its own demise?*

Once there lived an animal whose proportions were perfect, precisely suited for a quiet life, for roaming grassy spots near shore, gathering abundant fruits, seeds, roots, and nuts; who moved through its simple day in no hurry with no fear at all, in a place acknowledged as paradise. To find a name for such a creature, by which we might recognize others like it, to specialize innocence, classify unguardedness—we lost that chance long ago.

STUDY WITH
CRAPE MYRTLE

Say *Once there was a crape myrtle tree* . . . and right off it's a tale and it moves toward an end.

I know there are other ways of saying, like:

"What the hell *happened* at that moment . . . ?"

"Please let me never . . ."

"Still Life with Thing Indifferent to Me."

"To You Who Do Not Need My Eye to Complete You."

I've racked up here, as approaches go: inquiry, petition, title, dedication.

A simple letter, though, might be best, a form that both wanders and leads, weighs and allows for thoughts-come-upon. In the receptivity it assumes—a reader, you, settled into a comfortable chair, unsealing the envelope, unfolding the pages—a letter's a space where presence extends.

Dear,

A few weeks ago, on the way home with my dog, I took the street off to the side of the college. And there in the yard of the corner house was a spectacular crape myrtle. (The spelling varies: you'll see "crape" and "crepe"—though either way, the flowers aren't crinkly or ribbon-like.) A crape myrtle's deep-pink,

hardy blossoms cluster up like fat bunches of grapes. Maybe you
know that sketch by Picasso, *Hands Holding Flowers*, popular in
the '60s as an emblem of peace?—that bouquet-in-a-fist shows
exactly the blooms' angle of flare. The trunk's as smooth as the
arms of a girl, sleeveless in summer. But none of these images
came to me then—and none of this chatter.

Just, there it was.

And what filled that very long moment unfolding?

I should've been able to think *something*—to say *what a
beauty* or stopping short, at least give an *Oh* of surprise. But it
would not come forth as a specimen. "It" isn't right at all—and
there was the immediate problem: the tree would not be *called*
anything. Not "crape myrtle." Not even "tree." The simplest,
singular names weren't working. When I stopped and looked,
I heard just my own breathing. And being reduced to standing and breathing produced a wave of something fearsome.
Cliffs rose, the air sharpened and chilled between us. In the
steepness, I was unshimmed, root-cut, all pith. The tree sealed
itself up with—what? Solitude? A presence so insistently here,
it was ungrazed, unsnared, stripped clean—while I really
wasn't anywhere.

The tree in its quiet unspecialized me.

To have been pinned and bored into, gnawed back to a core,
to have felt myself splintering, or sharp-edged, would've helped.
But there was the tree. And there I was not. Not at the fringes.
Not in a web. Slipped from sight and in nothing's arms.

I hadn't expected this at all. I hadn't expected anything.

Certainly not to be dissolved by a tree. I was just out for a walk with my dog.

Yesterday, nearly a month later, I took down from my shelf Martin Buber's *I and Thou*, and when I opened the book (I haven't since college, the pages were dry and I had to endure my marginalia) it was to a highlighted sentence so absurdly exact— "I contemplate a tree"—that I laughed out loud.

Buber writes that while he could have, he did not "assign to it a species and observe it as an instance, with an eye to its construction and its way of life." He did not overcome its "uniqueness and form so rigorously that [he recognized] it only as an expression of the law." He did not "dissolve it into a number, into a pure relation between numbers, and eternalize it." The crape myrtle was, as he says of *his* tree, "no play of my imagination, no aspect of a mood"—and then, yes, "it confronts me bodily." Certain modes of apprehending, seeing, or contemplating (the taxonomizing of forms, for example), aren't *wrong*, Buber says—just not necessary, in order to be in relation to a tree. It's that *relation* is something different—a commodious state, disordered even.

And there was this, too: I felt if I didn't make something of the moment—the sight of the tree, what it did in me—the fearsomeness would evaporate (though I didn't exactly want to stay close to the not-being the tree kindled up). My desire to respond was powerful—and that desire, fully resisted. A gap opened up—as quick and sharp as a safety pin sprung. And my seeing-and-making was not sufficient. Not adequate-to. A puny gesture. Wind force–wise, I was a gnat in a Beaufort 8, where, the chart reads, "edges of crests break into spindrift, foam is blown in well-marked streaks"—walking against wind becomes very difficult. That's what it's been, these past months whenever I recall the scene.

How accustomed I am to being emplaced. To fashioning a place in words.

The height of the tree was not imposing. Nothing about its blossoms was weird, like flushed, pouty orchids beckoning *come, enter me here.* To have felt a part-of would've helped—to be the aphid that lives at the heart of those purple blossoms, a thing suited to its singular task, and built to participate in the mechanism of crape myrtle. But I was outside the composition. I had nothing to offer the closed system that was the tree. I remained unniched.

Recently I received a postcard from a friend (and just as I've been wrangling with making things—but I am growing more comfortable with extended forms of conversation with those I cannot see). He wrote: *I could spend my life making stuff no one cares about, not even me, really—except that I like making things. And going down to the hardware store, I was thinking how much I really liked that—just walking, being in the sun, alone. Just being in the sun alone. You know? How nice that is? How you can feel that's the whole reason to live. And it's enough.*

I know what he means—so often just to see a thing is steadying; to look on it is precisely enough: Rome, Via Appia, those dusty, resinous pine nuts on cobbles, and dew drying in chariot ruts; while ironing, the wrinkle in the landscape of a sleeve lying down like a time-lapse geological event; a just-picked fig, warm in the hand, heavy as an egg, with a sweet milky bead at the stem-tip. That day, though, when I angled toward home, when I turned and stopped looking, I could sense the tree going on being. And that made my seeing equal to ceasing, and the tree so much more than my speaking of it. Before this encounter, in another life, the moment might have been directly received; *oh, beautiful tree!* as sustaining and proper.

The emptying out of the form I knew as myself, the bright indifference of the tree, was shattering—but let me say (and how good it is that you're there on the other end), this impulse to make something of it all reconstitutes as I write to you.

I'll get to work, then, on a word for "the shattering calm that formlessness brings." For "the fear that accompanies invisibility." Or "a recognition that causes one to slip while standing still." "The bright air of ceasing, its watery savor," which if I had to name more precisely (I may have to write to you again on this) was something like a vein of iron, one I felt deep in me, as if banded in rock once lodged at the bottom of the sea, formed back at the beginning of the world as we know it—and which tastes (when swallowing hard, as one does when frightened or moved) uncorrupted, raw, free.

NOTES

"Scream (or Never Minding)": Quotes from Edvard Munch's journal are from Sue Prideaux's *Edvard Munch: Behind the Scream* (Yale University Press, 2005).

"My Eagles": Lewis Thomas quotes are from *Lives of a Cell: Notes of a Biology Watcher* (Norton, 1978). Eagle feather use information is from the White Earth Nation web site: www.whiteearth.com

"In the Despoiled and Radiant Now" is a line from Stephen Dunn's beautiful poem, "A Post-Mortem Guide" in *Different Hours* (Norton, 2000).

"All the Fierce Tethers": Christopher White's lucid illustrations of systems gone awry (in *The Melting World: A Journey Across America's Melting Glaciers*, St. Martin, 2013) and Ela Harrison's brilliant midrash informed this essay, as did Evelyn Fox Keller's *A Feeling for the Organism: the Life and Work of Barbara McClintock* (Henry Holt, 1983).

"Adventures in Beauty": This essay incorporates lines from Wallace Stevens ("Final Soliloquy of the Interior Paramour," Rainer Maria Rilke (*Duino Elegies*), John Keats ("Ode to a Grecian Urn").

"Brief Treatise Against Irony": *Zoom* information was found at en.wikipedia.org/wiki/zoom_1972_TV_series. I briefly quote Gerard Manley Hopkins' "Pied Beauty."

NOTES

"Walk with Snowy Things": This essay quotes Thomas Traherne's poem "My Spirit: Canto II."

"Bloodspots (I)": This essay quotes James Wright's poem "The Jewel."

"Bloodspots (III)": This essay quotes Emily Dickinson's poem #812, "A Light Exists in Spring" and Martin Buber's *I & Thou* (Charles Scribner's Sons, 1983, tr. Walter Kaufman).

ACKNOWLEDGMENTS

Thanks to the following publications and anthologies in which these essays first appeared sometimes in different form: *After Montaigne* (University of Georgia Press, 2015); *Agni*; *Brief Encounters: A Collection of Contemporary Nonfiction* (Norton, 2016); *Columbia: A Journal of Literature and the Arts*; *Ecotone*; *Georgia Review*; *Harvard Review*; *Iowa Review*; *The Journal*; *Las Sombras/The Shadows* (University of Texas Press, 2012); *The Literary House Press*; *New England Review*; *The Normal School*; *Orion*; *Pushcart Press Anthology XLI*; *Rooted: Best New Arboreal Nonfiction*; *See Double Press*; and *Trespass: Essayists Beyond the Boundaries of Place, Identity, and Feminism* (Lookout Books, 2019).

Much gratitude to the Guggenheim Foundation, the Dresher Center for the Humanities, and the Department of English at the University of Maryland, Baltimore County, and to the MacDowell Colony for their support of my work, and for the gifts of open, roaming time, and community.

And to Jed Gaylin, for holding while these words came into being. And to Sarah Gorham, whose vision lights the way. And to Kent Meyers, Brian Norman, Ann Pancake, and Wendy Willis, for reflecting back what emerged.

SARABANDE BOOKS is a nonprofit literary press located in Louisville, KY. Founded in 1994 to champion poetry, short fiction, and essay, we are committed to creating lasting editions that honor exceptional writing. For more information, please visit sarabandebooks.org.